CHRIST
AMONG OTHER gods

ERWIN W. LUTZER

MOODY PRESS
CHICAGO

ISBN: 0-8024-1649-7

3 5 7 9 10 8 6 4 2

Printed in the United States of America

To my parents, Gustav and Wanda Lutzer,
whose lives and words taught me early in life
that Christ was to be cherished
as the Son of God, the only Savior

About the Author

Erwin W. Lutzer (B.A., Winnipeg Bible College; Th.M., Dallas Theological Seminary; M.A., Loyola University; LL.D., Simon Greenleaf School of Law) is senior pastor of Moody Memorial Church, as well as a popular conference and radio speaker. He and his wife have three children.

CONTENTS

Foreword   7
Introduction   9

1. THE "GODS" ARE ON THE MOVE   11
   Have you caught the grand vision?

2. THE ICON OF TOLERANCE   27
   How did we get here?

3. THE SEARCH FOR TRUTH   43
   If it's true for me, is it true for you?

4. AN EXTRAORDINARY BIRTH   61
   What does it take to be a savior?

5. AN EXTRAORDINARY LIFE   79
   Who is the real Jesus?

6. AN EXTRAORDINARY AUTHORITY   97
   If God has spoken, what has He said?

7. AN EXTRAORDINARY DEATH   115
   What happened on that middle cross?

8. AN EXTRAORDINARY RESURRECTION   131
   Could the disciples have made up the story?

9. AN EXTRAORDINARY ASCENSION   147
   What is Christ doing today?

10. AN EXTRAORDINARY RETURN   163
    Which God reigns?

11. AN EXTRAORDINARY STUMBLING BLOCK   179
    Is everyone else lost?

12. AN EXTRAORDINARY RESPONSIBILITY   195
    How can we best represent Him?

FOREWORD

People with no ear for music say that it all sounds the same, but lovers of Bach, Handel, Beethoven, and Brahms know better. So, too, people who lack spiritual concern or factual knowledge or both tell us that the world's religions are really all the same, and one is as good as another, so that it does not matter which is yours. They also are wrong, however, as Christians clearly see.

The figure of Jesus Christ, as portrayed in the gospel history and shown forth in the rest of the New Testament, is unique. A Man who acted, as Jesus did, like God come in the flesh; who spoke of Himself as the Son of God; who identified Himself as future judge of the world and arbiter of everyone's destiny; who, after being crucified, came alive from the dead, leaving His tomb and graveclothes empty, and met His disciples again; who, having entered the world by a miraculous conception and birth, and fulfilled in it a miraculous ministry, even to raising the dead, was seen to leave it by a miraculous ascension; and whose disciples for two thousand years have been sure that He actually shares their life, as they share His; why, no other religious leader, and no other religious experience, has ever been remotely like this! As a faith founded on unique supernatural facts, and as a unique, life-changing relationship with its unique divine Founder, Christianity is truly a unique religion. This fact ought to be beyond dispute.

In these days, however, the unique glory of Christ and His ministry to those who trust Him have to be constantly highlighted, for our multi-religious world is going through a bad patch of failing to distinguish things that differ. Erwin Lutzer's forthright restatement of what everyone needs to know about Jesus in the context of the world's religions is therefore a book to be welcomed. God bless it!

J. I. PACKER
Vancouver, B. C.

INTRODUCTION

At a time when interest in Christ is increasing, it is no secret that the world's religions are growing at an unprecedented
rate in the United States. Although Christianity has historically
insisted on its uniqueness, many religious leaders are predicting that the problems of the world are becoming so formidable
that religious unity will be inevitable in the not so distant future.

Never before have I written a book with such a burden, a
growing conviction that as we march toward the next century it
is absolutely essential that we as believers not only have Christ
in our hearts but also in our heads. We must be able to invite
others to investigate Christ's claims without embarrassment or
fear that the evidence for our faith will evaporate. We need answers for ourselves and others in a day when religious truth has
been reclassified as little more than personal opinions and private experiences.

I want to thank my friend Ravi Zacharias for allowing me to
use the title *Christ Among Other gods* in the publication of this
book. Several years ago I heard a message of his entitled, "Jesus
Among Other gods," and it stuck in my mind. Although the content of this book is wholly mine, I wrote to Ravi asking whether I
could be given the option of using a version of his title and he

graciously agreed. I'm thankful for his friendship and rejoice in his effective and worldwide ministry.

Thanks to the members and friends of the Moody Church who heard the essential contents of this book delivered as a series of messages in the fall of 1993. Though it has been my privilege to preach from this historic pulpit for fifteen years, I have never grown weary of the work nor taken this honor for granted. Thanks to the prayers of God's people, I have been blessed with the opportunity of serving Christ beyond the walls of Moody Church through speaking and writing.

A special word of thanks to my administrative assistant, Pauline Epps, who spent many hours formatting the manuscript and making helpful suggestions along the way. And most important, I give loving appreciation to my wife Rebecca and our three daughters, Lori, Lynn, and Lisa, who were so understanding during the days when this book was uppermost on my mind and kept me in my study.

All praise goes to my Lord and Savior Jesus Christ whom I love and in whose defense this book has been written. My greatest reward would be that those who read it would love Him more, worship Him more fervently, and defend Him with conviction and grace.

THE
"GODS" ARE
ON THE MOVE—

Have You Caught the Grand Vision?

"Unite or Perish!"

That message seemed to dominate every session of the Parliament of the World's Religions that met in Chicago in 1993. And the group most often targeted for criticism—the folks who could not be expected to buy into this united agenda—were those who belonged to the historic Christian faith. I'm convinced that a religious tidal wave is sweeping America; the message I heard at the parliament was that we had better get on board or be left to swim (or drown) on our own!

The gods are on a roll, and woe to those who stand in the way of their agenda! With lofty ideals and utopian plans to unify the religions of the world for the common good, this parliament met to break down the barriers that exist in the accelerated march toward unity. Six thousand delegates came to learn from one another, explore areas of agreement, and grasp a better understanding of one another's religious heritages. They also promoted a global ethic designed to alleviate the suffering and wars of the world. Their time, they say, has come.

What place did Christ have in the more than 700 workshops that were available during the eight-day conference? At times He was variously admired, quoted, and favorably compared to other religious teachers, ancient and modern. He was seen as one more stage in the evolutionary development of religion; indeed, He was a very necessary and important stage, but He was only one enlightened man among many. It was noted that in our day He is overshadowed by others but that He should be admired for being the man for *His* times. A *special* man for His times.

Except for one or two speakers (one said of Him, "He didn't even know the world was round"), Christ was thus revered for His contribution in the history of religion. He was even described by some as a revealer of God, a man who had achieved the highest degree of enlightenment. Others allowed that He was the Master of Masters, the one who shows us the way; the one who is to be loved and followed. But alas, He was only one among many others. Though He was *respected,* He was not *worshiped.*

What I saw and heard in Chicago is a microcosm of your school, business, and community. The people who live next door and your associates at work most likely believe that it doesn't matter what god you pray to because every deity is ultimately the same deity shrouded in a different name. According to the 1993–94 Barna research report, nearly two out of three adults contend that the choice of one religious faith over another is irrelevant because all religions teach the same basic lessons about life.[1]

Perhaps you belong to that majority, and if so I invite you to compare Christ with other religious options. Join me on a journey that will investigate His claims, assess the historical records, and examine whether He should just be admired or actually worshiped. I'm not writing about a hidden Christ who is accessible only to those who already believe; as best I can, I present a Christ whose credentials are open for thoughtful investigation. If you think that all the deities are the same, or that all religions agree on the essential points, this book is for you.

And if you already are a Christian, I want to sound a wake-up call, an opportunity to join a growing number of believers who have chosen to sink their roots deeper, to understand their faith better, and to turn their beliefs into convictions. We should be glad for the opportunity to represent Christ in our pluralistic age. This is not a time to hide the light in our hearts but to let it shine in the hazy dusk of religious pluralism. Never before has it been so important to have Christ in our heads and not just in our hearts!

Have we—I speak to those of us who are committed Christians—have we become so desensitized by the tolerance of our age that we can see Christ dethroned in the minds of multitudes and turn away as if we didn't notice? We all remember how dismayed Christians became when the movie "The Last Temptation of Christ" was released. Yet we don't realize that a similar desecration happens whenever Christ is classified as just one among many options.

Yes, of course we believe that eventually "at the name of Jesus every knee should bow, of those who are in heaven, and on earth, and under the earth, and that every tongue should confess that Jesus Christ is Lord, to the glory of God the Father" (Philippians 2:10–11), but we must rekindle our passion for Him to be honored in our day among our neighbors and friends. Our love for Him can be measured by our concern about His reputation among the people of the world.

Now if Christ is indeed only one among many; if He is but one of the gods, then it is time for all the religions of the world to unite. Let all religious leaders stand on equal ground; let them pool their insights so that they can fight our battles with a unified army. Enough of division! Enough of fruitless arguments! Enough of bigotry!

Which forces the question: Does Christ belong on the same shelf with Buddha, Krishna, Bahá ú lláh, and Zoroaster? Like Christ, such leaders (and others) have taught some rather lofty ethical ideas. Even if we say He stands taller than the rest, have we given Him His due? Or is He to be placed on an entirely different shelf altogether? That, of course, is the subject of this book.

Mind you, at the parliament no one suggested that Christians should stop being Christians or that Hindus should stop being Hindus; nor should Buddhists stop being Buddhists. The religions of the world have a rich diversity that should be prized.

Each should be admired as one beautiful petal; together they form a magnificent flower called religion, a flower that no one religion could create by itself.

This flower is growing more quickly before our eyes than we realize. The soil has been prepared, the seeds have been planted, and the plant is beginning to bloom. Only mindless fanatics would spoil its beauty and energy. This flower, we are told, will bless the world.

THE FOUNDATION FOR UNITY

This is not a book about the Parliament of the World's Religions, though I shall refer to what happened there to illustrate how Christ is viewed in our culture. Nor is it a book on comparative religions, since such subjects have already been adequately treated by others. This book is about Christ; it is an attempt to understand Him better, worship Him more, and represent Him with more confidence. But first we have to cover some important matters to set the context for the discussion.

I attended the parliament because I wanted to learn more about the religions of the world, to have a better grasp of the complexity we face in America today. Second, I wanted to meet as many people as possible, to compare their beliefs with those of Christ (a few of these stories are in this book). Third, I wanted to look through the window of prophecy to see the formation of a worldwide religious system which, in all probability, will be the basis of Antichrist's brief rule on planet earth.

The premises that were either directly stated or implied in every session have already taken root in our culture. Listen to our talk shows, read the newspapers, or attend the local school board meeting and you will find these views widely accepted and seldom challenged.

1. The doctrines of the different faiths should not be held as truths but as shells that contain kernels that are found in all religions. Since the claim for truth is a stumbling block to unity, it is best to speak of religious *traditions* rather than religious *truths.*

2. No religion should be thought of as superior to another. Indeed, this belief in superiority is the major roadblock to religious unity. At the parliament, seminars were held to overcome "this crucial obstacle."

3. We can retain our own particular religion but must move beyond it to deeper levels of experience. As we move away from religion to this true spirituality, we are united.

4. Proselytizing (Christians call it *evangelism*) is bigotry, pure and simple. The idea of winning converts is based on the antiquated notion that one religion has more to offer than another. Our task is to help others discover the hidden inner meaning of their religions, rather than convert them to our own.

To quote the words of Swami Chindanansa of the Divine Life Society, "There are many effective, equally valid religions. They are to be equally reverenced, equally recognized, and equally loved and cherished—not merely tolerated. The Hindu Scriptures say, 'In whatever way men approach Me, even so do I go to them.'"[2] But if the different religions are the same in essence, why do they appear so disparate to us? *It's all a matter of perspective;* how easy it is for all of us to give a different description of the same thing. God (or the gods) is one; it is our fallible interpretations that bring disunity.

At the parliament, the delegates were often led to shout "I AM!" as an affirmation of their own godhood. People who still believed in prayer were told that they should pray to their own "god of choice." We were told that the better we understand ourselves and our global village, the more readily we will be mature enough to realize that no religion has a right to exclusivity. Some gods may work best for you; whereas the rich traditions of the goddesses are more appealing to your friends.

THE VISION OF UNITY

The famous historian, Arnold Toynbee, predicted that the governments of the world would unite either by force or federation, but that the unity could not succeed without a universal religion. Christianity, he said, should be purged of its "sinful state of mind," namely, its exclusivism. The political/economic framework of world government needs to be supported by the unified spiritual dimension of humankind.[3]

This appears to be happening before our eyes. As America has become more diversified racially, so it is becoming more diversified religiously. We are told that the only hope for peaceful co-existence in our country and the larger world is for the religions of the world to set aside their differences and rally around the common banner of love, acceptance, and service to our fellow man. After all, the various religions are but different expressions of the same ultimate, the same god (or gods).

Listen to some of the benefits unity will bring:

— An end to war

— An end to hunger through a redistribution of the world's resources and population control

— Conservation of the earth's environment

— Genuine equality among all races and religions and between men and women

— A global ethic that will unite the human family

— The dawn of an entirely new age of human achievement and potential

Later in this book I shall discuss what will happen to those who do not sign on to this agenda. Evidently all of us will soon have to make up our minds because by the year 2000, we are told, the transformation will be well on its way.

Testimonies—scores of them—were given about the personal benefits of those who have taken the time to harmonize the rational mindset of the religious West with the mystical experience of the religious East. Religious unity will change the world because it begins by changing individuals.

One woman claimed healing through mystical meditation; another said her New Age religion saved her marriage. One man said that only when he delved into Hinduism did he "find the other half of his soul." Words often used were "fulfillment," "peace," or "energy." Yes, there were plenty of testimonials to say, "It works!"

ILLUSTRATIONS OF UNITY

In John Godfrey Saxe's well-known poem "The Blind Men and the Elephant," the six blind men of Indostan all wanted to learn what an elephant was like. Each approached the beast from a different direction; each explored part of the elephant— its side, its tusk, its trunk, its leg, its ear, and its tail. Relating their experiences, the six compared the elephant to a wall, a spear, a snake, a tree, a fan, and a rope.

> And so these men of Indostan
> Disputed loud and long,
> Each in his own opinion
> Exceeded stiff and strong
> Though each was partly in the right
> And all were in the wrong!
>
> So, oft in theologic wars
> The disputants, I ween,
> Rail on in utter ignorance
> Of what each other mean,
> And prate about an elephant
> Not one of them has seen![4]

If only we would realize that the various religions of the world are simply different aspects of the same divinity! In fact, the argument goes, we should be thankful for these diverse ways of seeing because they give us a fuller picture of whatever gods or goddesses there be. Far from thinking that one religion is superior, we should expand our horizons to see the bigger picture. The Religious Ultimate is greater than any one portrait of him or her.

If the blind men and the elephant illustrate why we have different religious traditions, the wheel helps us understand what happens when we move away from our dogmas and unite the core of our beliefs. Visualize a wheel with a rim, spokes, and hub. At (1) the outer rim we find our different religious doctrines, which form the most superficial level of understanding; but, (2) once we grasp that our beliefs are symbols, we begin to move toward the center. At the rim, dialogue is impossible because it is even difficult for us to understand how other people believe as they do; but as we move toward the center, we find a deeper meaning. Then, (3) finally at the hub we discover our true unity; here is "the brilliant blue of empty sky" as I heard one person put it. Now we can better appreciate other religions, because we see them through the lens of inner unity and faith.

OBSTACLES TO UNITY

But what should we do with our doctrinal beliefs, those stubborn convictions that are roadblocks to unity? In one session of the parliament one leader said, "Hold on to your chairs tightly, as if you might go through the ceiling if you were to let go. Now think of one of your most cherished beliefs—now let go of both your chair and your cherished belief! Nothing happened, right? Now you've got the feel of it!" Then we were told that we could have our belief back, thank you very much. We just have to get used to "letting go!"

If we still struggle with "letting go" of our cherished beliefs there was a seminar titled, "A Vocabulary for the 21st Century," which aimed to show that all so-called doctrines were merely metaphors for a deeper meaning. In practical terms, this means that one can give up his doctrines without surrendering the terminology that communicates them. The Bible, it was said, does not mean what most think it does; all that is required is to give up our doctrines and then we will see that its metaphors will yield a deeper, hidden meaning. If only we could progress beyond the childish stages of our faith and grow to maturity, to *inclusive* maturity.

Christianity, we're told, had failed—at least the form common in the Western world. We have squandered the earth's resources because of the foolish notion that we should have dominion over the earth. Christianity talks of love and breeds hate; it speaks of one creator yet divides the creation with its narrow doctrines. The message was clear: It's time to move on. Christianity is like a boat that has taken us across the river; now it's time to abandon it for the exciting new future. We are leaving the Piscean Age (Christianity) for the age of Aquarius. Goodbye to the past and welcome to the future!

Well, I think you've got the picture. When someone says that Christianity has failed, most people interpret that to mean that Christ has failed. It's our Savior they are talking about! And it is our privilege to help the world see that they might just be mistaken in their assessment.

Two immediate questions come to mind: How is the Bible viewed when a spirit of ecumenism (inclusiveness) takes over? And where does Christ fit within a syncretistic (religiously unified) culture?

What About the Bible?

Obviously if the Bible is to harmonize with any number of religious viewpoints, it has to be reinterpreted, made to "fit" if you please. Whenever I've been on a talk show or have debated the merits of Christ, I've heard, "That's just *your* interpretation!" The impression is given that the Bible can be easily stripped of its literal meaning and made compatible with any number of viewpoints.

Now that the attempt to unify the religions of the world is serious business, a new book entitled *The Bible Illuminated* has just been released. It is a collection of Bible stories (from both Old and New Testaments) that interprets these accounts from a universal standpoint. The editor/author of the book is Swami Bhaktipada who says his goal is "to give Christians and those of other faiths an understanding of the Bible that is not sectarian, to encourage an appreciation of the Bible as a particular expression of the eternal truth that is taught in all the world's great religious traditions."[5]

The Bible Illuminated, which comes with 101 mystical paintings, is part of a series of books designed to show that all the religions of the world have essential unity. Already the Swami has published *The Illustrated Ramayana*, an English edition of the Hindu Vedic scriptures. To quote him once more, "A true devotee, whether or not he is a Christian, Muslim, Jew, Hindu or of another faith, is inspired by the hearing of the Lord's glories from any authorized source—from David's Psalms or Lord Krishna's Gita, from the Ramayana or the Koran."[6]

Reality is always obscure, but because we abhor ambiguity, we tend to hold tenaciously to our own point of view. But as we mature and are able to synthesize the various perspectives, we unify our viewpoints. Eventually, the greater the unity, the greater the clarity of vision.

So much for the Bible.

What About Christ?

Standing in the way of the Grand Plan for religious unity is the person of Christ. Historically, Christianity has held Him to be unique, the only special Son of God, the Lord, Savior. But many Christians—or at least many of those who use the label—are beginning to think that we can no longer maintain exclusivity in the midst of the growing awareness of other faiths. And the push to unity is too powerful, too inviting to resist.

Here are three possible ways to relate Christ to the challenges of other religions.

First, there is *pluralism*—the direct assertion that we must accept all religions as equals. Christ is only a man, a prophet, one of a variety of options, and not necessarily a better option at that. Pluralism insists that even the word *tolerance* smacks of bigotry, the insinuation that we have to "tolerate" those who are different from us. We should not simply tolerate different religions; we should grant them the same respect we give our own. In this scenario Christ is variously interpreted, but always He is stripped of His deity (unless His assertions are interpreted to mean that all of us are divine).

This pluralism (or universalism) affirms without qualification that no religion has the right to sit in judgment upon another. Without mutual respect, uncritical tolerance, and an unqualified acceptance of the rich heritage of others, there are no grounds for unity. Superiority leads to the prejudice that must be exposed, despised, and eventually plucked up by the roots.

A second more common stance is *inclusivism*—an openness to other religions that began with the eighteenth-century Enlightenment. Christ, in this view, may still be unique, but He does not have sole possession of the truth. Other religions are also an expression of the divine, though their form may be less clear than that given to us in the New Testament.

Liberals have always sought to demonstrate the spiritual value of other religions. The World Council of Churches stresses that only through religious dialogue amid the diversity of the world's religions is it possible to see the totality of God's revelation. Only ignorance and narrow-mindedness would limit God's revelation to Christianity, the dominant religion of the West.

Since Vatican II, this march toward inclusivism has been seen in the Catholic Church too. Previously, it was fervently believed that salvation could come only through the church—that is, the Catholic Church. But now that Protestants are called "separated brethren," one text of the Council says that the Roman Church must no longer be identified as the sole church of Jesus Christ and "that those who have not yet received the Gospel are related to the Church in various ways."[7] Interestingly, now that the door of salvation has opened to Protestants, it has also opened for those of other religions. Pope John Paul has been known to pray with Hindus, Buddhists, and representatives of other faiths.

Third, there is *exclusivism* which maintains that God has revealed Himself only in Christ; all other religions are therefore incomplete, misleading, and false. Elijah, the mighty prophet of the Old Testament, one might call an exclusivist. When he had a contest with the prophets of Baal and they were proven to be false, he took 400 of them and had them put to death at the river Kishon.

The New Testament continues with this tradition of exclusivity, except that followers of other religions are no longer subject to civil penalties. (Although intermittently throughout the history of the church heretics were burned at the stake, this was based on a confusion between the Old Testament age and the New Testament command to render to Caesar that which is Caesar's and to God that which is God's.)

Exclusivism, I might add, does not conflict with freedom of religion. Freedom to adopt whatever religion one wishes (or none at all) should be a right in all countries, especially those that have been influenced by the Christian faith. As we shall see later, a proper definition of exclusivism means that, whereas we recognize and respect freedom of religion, we do not compromise our beliefs. We also do not combine them with other religions or philosophies. If there is one true God, our options are limited.

These three possibilities spawn other variations. For example, there is *selectivism* which says that we must not follow any one religion but compile our own personal list of cherished beliefs. A smorgasbord has the advantage of having many nourishing items, and we get to choose whatever suits our fancy. This is more democratic, more in keeping with the radical individualism that is so highly prized in America. In such a context, Christ can play any role you want Him to.

Increasingly our generation wants to take religion out of the realm of rational discourse and relegate it to the area of personal preferences and opinions. If there are thirty-one flavors of ice cream, why can we not have similar variety in religions? The gods of the New Age Movement are always tolerant of sexual preferences, feminism, and hedonistic pleasures at almost any cost. Why shouldn't we each choose a religion that is compatible with our private values? In order to have a meaningful faith, it must agree with our deeply held beliefs. What works for you might not work for me.

What About You?

Interest in Christ is on the rise. A recent article in *U.S. News & World Report* says that "the quest for the historical Jesus is getting a new surge of scholarly energy."[8] Every day—in churches, in self-help groups, in discussions at home and in the office—Christ is discussed. In fact, interest in Him seems to be increasing right along with the proliferation of new species of privatized religion. Christ is being redefined to suit the syncretism of our times. Later I'll explain why many who speak well of Him actually are undermining His credibility.

I've discovered that the less some people know about Christ the more they like Him. The baby in the manger touches even the most cynical soul who has long since given up on religion. The secularist who is bent on reforming society quotes selected verses from the Sermon on the Mount with reverence. And the religious types use Him as their example of humility, sacrifice, and basic goodness. He is worthy to be spoken about in hushed tones. He is, say some, the first among equals. Yet in all this He is often dammed by faint praise.

Since Christ said that the world would hate Him, we can be quite sure that *when the world loves Him it is because they have made Him into something He is not.* The biblical Christ cannot be dismissed; He stands in our path forcing us to make a decision, either to the right or to the left. In His presence neutrality is impossible. The babe in the manger quickly grows to become God, the King.

THE PURPOSE OF THIS BOOK

I've written this book to give reasons why Christ must always stand alone; all attempts to unite Him with the religions of the world are doomed to fail. Once we clarify His credentials and the gospel He brought us, we will realize that the Christian faith is exclusive and must logically be so. Amid charges of bigotry, our task is to be lovingly exclusive. If there is any good news in this world, the followers of Christ will have to proclaim it.

The Bible draws a definitive line through the peoples of the world, but it is not a line between races, nations, or even cultures, as such. This line separates Christ and His followers from all other religious choices. I'm committed to helping us identify that line, show where it should be drawn, and give reasons that we have no right to move it.

FBI agents, I am told, don't spend much time studying counterfeit money since there are too many varieties of bogus bills. Rather, they study the genuine articles, observing all their unique details. Armed with a good knowledge of authentic money, they can recognize counterfeits of whatever kind. Those who are conversant with the truth recognize error when they see it.

I've already mentioned that this book is a study about Christ against the backdrop of other religious preferences. If we take a careful look at the genuine article, namely the God-man, we will recognize other teachers who have a different origin and belief. I intend to show why although other religions take bad men and try to make them better, *only one is qualified to take dead men and make them alive.*

When you travel through Switzerland, you often see two mountains in the distance that appear to be joined, but as you get closer you may find that they are separated by very sheer cliffs. And down below is a fast-flowing, uncrossable river.

Take a superficial look at Christ and other gods and you might think that there are some impressive similarities. Take a closer look and you will discover that they are separated by an unbridgeable chasm. Christ has little in common with other teachers, prophets, Swamis, and gurus. It is not just that He stands taller than others; in His presence they disappear somewhere beyond the horizon.

Christians are not called to wring their hands when pagan ideas dilute the truths of the gospel. We are called to give a credible response, to raise His banner, and to expect that at least some people will salute. I hope you share my passion to know Christ with such accuracy, to be convinced of His credentials with such certainty, and to see His uniqueness with such clarity that we will be able to present Him to anyone, regardless of his or her religion of choice.

Here are some comments you have heard from your friends or on talk shows. Or maybe you hold one of these opinions yourself. Either way, my intention is to help us clarify why such views are based on a major misunderstanding of Christ:

— "You're into Christ . . . I'm into Buddha . . . we all have to choose the religion that is best for us."

— "I love Christ as much as you do, but I don't think He is the only way to God. . . . God would never limit the way to heaven to one person. My God is more inclusive than that . . ."

— "I think that much of the New Testament contains mythology. I don't believe these things happened. It's just a matter of interpretation."

— "I think that all the religions of the world are essentially the same; why should we argue about the peripheral matters?"

— "I haven't left my Christianity, I've just moved beyond it to something deeper. I no longer emphasize religion but am into spirituality . . ."

An artist named Gustave Doré completed a painting of Christ. A passerby paused to admire his work and remarked, "You must love Him to paint Him so well!" The artist replied, "Yes, I do love Him, but if I loved Him more, I'd paint Him better!"

Eight chapters in this book are devoted to painting a verbal portrait of Christ. As best I can, I have shown His uniqueness and pointed out why all attempts to link Him with others are misguided. Having made this study, I love Him more, and I'm praying that when you have finished reading what I've written, you also will love Him more so that together we can "paint Him better!"

But before I begin the portrait, the next chapter explains where we are as a culture and why presenting Christ's message has its special challenges in our day. Then another chapter will be devoted to the question of religious truth, answering the objections of those who believe that all religions lead to the same end. I'll show why the illustration of the wheel (referred to above) is so profoundly wrongheaded.

Then we begin our journey, placing Christ on the shelf with other gods. Can the gods compete? Or do they topple like the ancient Philistine god Dagon when placed next to the ark of the Lord—helpless in the presence of Someone much greater than they? (1 Samuel 5:3).

Read on.

NOTES

1. George Barna, *Absolute Confusion,* (Ventura, Calif.: Regal Books, 1993), 15.
2. Swami Chindanansa, "Authentic Religion" a paper distributed at the Parliament of World Religions.
3. Arnold Toynbee, *Christianity Among the Religions of the World* (New York: Charles Scribner's Sons, 1957), 95f.
4. From *The Best Loved Poems of the American People,* selected by Hazel Felleman (New York: Doubleday & Co., 1936), 522.
5. Advertisement of Palace Publishing, distributed at The Parliament Of World Religions.
6. Ibid.
7. A. P. Flannery, ed., *Documents of Vatican II* (Grand Rapids: Eerdmans, 1975), 367.
8. *U.S. News & World Report,* 20 December 1993, 62.

THE
ICON OF
TOLERANCE—

How Did We Get Here?

Have you ever seen a god?

Years ago when I visited Baalbeck near Beirut, Lebanon, I actually saw the ancient god Baal. He (or it) was chiseled out of solid stone, with a grim smile on his otherwise expressionless face. Though I have never returned, I have the suspicion that he still looks the same as he did when I was there more than twenty-five years ago.

Though you and I have never chiseled a god out of stone, we all face the strong temptation of remaking our idea of God to conform to our image. Freud argued that the hopes and dreams of humans resemble the alleged characteristics of "God" so closely that people simply transfer their hopes and wishes to an imaginary being. Karl Marx agreed that man makes religion; religion does not make man. Man has "found only his reflection in the fantastic reality of heaven, where he sought a supernatural being."

In her book *A History of God,* Karen Armstrong argues that God is indeed a product of humankind's creative imagination. God, she says, may well be our most interesting idea. She claims that Yahweh (Hebrew for Jehovah) was originally a savage, partisan god of war and one of several deities worshiped by the Israelites. It took seven centuries for this unpleasant being to evolve into the Almighty Yahweh proclaimed by the prophets as the one and only God. New ideas about God have always emerged in response to new psychological needs. In fact, she thinks that if the great faiths did not have the capacity to change, they might well have withered away. Consequently, each generation has to create its own imaginative conception of God.[1]

So, does God create man or has man created God? Paul taught that men and women often create gods according to their own liking. The pagans exchanged "the glory of the incorruptible God for an image in the form of corruptible man and of birds and four-footed animals and crawling creatures" (Romans 1:23). Yes, individuals and cultures can create gods.

Our highly specialized, consumer-oriented society has redefined God so that He no longer stands in judgment of our culture but rather endorses it. According to the book, *The Day America Told the Truth,* the word *God* to most Americans is "a distant and pale reflection of the God of their forefathers. . . . This is not the 'jealous God' of the Old Testament but . . . a general sense of good and happiness in the world."[2] And someone has said that heaven for modern man looks like the biggest shopping mall one can imagine. We have a god who desires our pleasure, a god (or goddess, if you prefer) who promotes feminism, sexual preferences, abortion, and radical individualism. We have a god who is wholly committed to our happiness and who believes in human potential. We have a god who lets us make up our own ten commandments.

For such a kinder, gentler god to flourish, we have had to bow before another god who is undisturbed by the moral/spiritual/religious diversity in our culture. This god's name is *tolerance.* Officially, sin does not exist in our society, but if there were one sin left it would be a belief in objective truth, a belief that some things are still right or wrong; a belief that discrimination still has value if defined as being discriminating in what we believe, the way we behave, and what we defend.

"To live and let live" has now been enshrined as the one non-negotiable absolute of society. Only what is often defined as intolerance is utterly intolerable. Our God is as tolerant as a talk show host, as loving as a doting grandparent, and, I might add, as relevant as last year's calendar.

Let me be clear that tolerance can be defined in two legitimate ways. As mentioned in the first chapter, *legal tolerance* is the right for everyone to believe in whatever faith (or none at all) he wishes. Such tolerance is very important in our society, and we as Christians should maintain our conviction that no one should ever be coerced into believing as we do. Freedom of religion should not only be retained in Western democracies but promoted in other countries as well.

Second, there is *social tolerance,* a commitment to respecting all men even if we vigorously disagree with their religion and ideas. When we engage other religions and moral issues in the ideological marketplace, it should be with courtesy and kindness. We must live in peace with all men and women, even with those of divergent faiths, or those who have no faith at all. We don't need any more self-righteous Christians who piously judge others without the humble admission that we are all a part of a fallen human race; we are all imperfect and we are all created in the image of God. Tolerance, like patience, is a fruit of the Holy Spirit.

But the tolerance of which I speak—our national icon, if you will—is something quite different. This is an *uncritical tolerance* that avoids vigorous debate in the quest for truth. This new tolerance insists that we have no right to disagree with a liberal social agenda; we should not defend our views of morality, religion, and respect for human life. This tolerance respects absurd ideas but will castigate anyone who believes in absolutes or who claims to have found some truth. This tolerance, someone has said, includes every point of view except those points of view that do not include every point of view. This is tolerance only for those who march in step with the tolerant crowd.

This new god is our one absolute, the one flag still deemed worthy of our honor. This kind of tolerance is used as an excuse for perpetual skepticism, for keeping any religious commitment at arm's length; it is also a doorway for being vulnerable to accept the most bizarre ideas. Truth, it is assumed, might exist in mathematics and science, but not in religion or morality. The pressure to accept this uncritical tolerance is growing every year.

You've heard of "political correctness," that doctrine based on a new American right—the right to never be offended. If your views run counter to the official liberal agenda, it is best to remain quiet or be accused of "verbal violence." Rules are being made to prohibit any speech that is offensive to a minority group. Needless to say, pro-lifers are an offense to many people; so are those who do not believe in the homosexual agenda; so are those who believe that Christ is the only way to God.

"The purpose of education," laments Allan Bloom, "is not to make scholars but provide them with a moral virtue—openness."[3] He says that reason has been replaced by mindless commitment, "an exercise in consciousness-raising, trashy sentimentality and elevated sentiment."[4] The quest for truth is short-circuited because truth, if it exists at all, is beyond our reach.

We have moved from the conviction that everyone has a right to his own opinions to the notion that every opinion is equally right! We have moved from genuine pluralism, the idea that the religions of the world can peacefully co-exist, to syncretism, the idea that the beliefs of various religions can be mindlessly combined.

If you were on a talk show and said, "I believe in Christ," you would be applauded; but if you were to say "Christ is the Savior for everyone," boos would echo throughout the crowd. At the Parliament of the World's Religions, a seminar was held to show that the Jordan River and the Ganges River actually are the same religious stream. Christ and Krishna, the perfect team!

How did we get to this point in American history? How did we arrive at the idea that mathematics, science, and history are in the category of rational truth, but morality and religion should be relegated to matters of personal taste and private experience? What conditions in society have made it possible for some people to believe contradictory or even absurd ideas? The purpose of this chapter is:

1. To glance in the rear view mirror to better understand where we have come from, ideologically speaking, and where we are headed. There are reasons that the search for truth has ended with a sigh and hopeless resignation that each person's opinion is just as right as anyone else's.

2. To understand how the ideas of our culture have affected the evangelical churches in America. We may angrily dispute the notion that every generation creates its own God, but the humbling fact is that our idea of God—yes, even the Christian God—has also been shaped by the prevailing culture.

THE IDEOLOGICAL MEGASHIFT

Our nation has experienced an ideological shift of titanic proportions. We act differently than our forefathers because we think differently. As a nation we have given up the search for values, and worse, we no longer believe that such values exist. Where did we get off track?

I'll explain this megashift by listing five characteristics of modern thinking. These changes have not taken place in neat stages nor have they happened in sequence. But as we shall see, all of these ideological currents are related; one leads inevitably to another, creating an ever-widening stream. All of us are affected; the end to which they lead should drive us to our knees.

God-Centered Worldview to Man-Centeredness

Two hundred years after the Reformation of the sixteenth century, Europe experienced the Enlightenment. I visited Goethe's house in Weimar, Germany, and was impressed with the artifacts from all over the world, particularly Greece and Rome but also China and Japan. Goethe appreciated art, of course, but he also wanted to make a theological statement: Other religions, even pagan religions, can produce a culture as advanced as Christianity. Therefore, Christianity should not be thought of as having any special place in the history of the race but should be studied as one of many helpful religions.

When man saw himself as the center of all knowledge, he defined religion according to his own expectations and desires. Religion was no longer thought of as the quest for man to rightly adjust his life to the demands of God, but as a system of beliefs that helps him achieve his full potential.

A noted historian, Joseph Haroutunian, remarks:

> Before, religion was God-centered. Before, whatever was not conducive to the glory of God was infinitely evil; now that which is not conducive to the happiness of man is evil, unjust, and impossible to attribute to the deity. Before, the good of man consisted ultimately in glorifying God; now the glory of God consists in the good of man. Before, man lived to glorify God; now God lived to serve man.[5]

The Enlightenment was not opposed to religion; it simply declared that our knowledge of God should not come through the Bible but through the universal light of nature. As such all religions of the world were essentially equal, based as they were on natural observation and experience. The Bible was seen as a helpful book, but it was not considered a revelation from a personal God. Human reason was elevated above revelation.

The Enlightenment was a mixed blessing. On the one hand it did emphasize religious freedom and tolerance in the best sense of the word. Two centuries earlier, the Reformation had breathed new spiritual life into parts of Europe. This light, however, was often smothered, if not extinguished, by the religious controversies that followed years later. We can understand why people were fed up with the intolerance of the era. The Enlightenment brought a much needed emphasis on freedom of learning and freedom of conscience.

But unfortunately, the Enlightenment also ushered in deep darkness. When Germany (and all of Europe, for that matter) chose to opt for that kinder, gentler theology referred to earlier, the gospel of Christ was obscured. Man became the judge of religion and morality, and despite noble ideals, darkness— deep darkness—descended.

Crimes committed in the name of religion (and there were many) pale into insignificance in comparison to the crimes committed in the name of an atheistic view of man and the world. It is not simply a historical accident that Buchenwald, one of Hitler's concentration camps, is only six kilometers from Weimar—an irony which evidently was not lost on Der Fuhrer. He had, I am told, perverted delight in setting up a death camp just outside the borders of the city that prided itself in tolerance and the glory of man.

It is a scandal beyond irony that when men throw off the disciplines of revealed religion, their freedom ends in slavery. Religious tyranny must, of course, be abhorred; but when mankind uses its coveted freedom to disown God, a worse tyranny follows.

When Solzenitsyn was asked how it could be that so many millions of people were brutally put to death under the banner of atheism, he answered simply, "We have forgotten God." Dostoevsky was right, "When God does not exist, everything is permitted."

Speaking of false teachers, Peter writes, " . . . promising them freedom while they themselves are slaves of corruption; for by what a man is overcome, by this he is enslaved" (2 Peter 2:19).

This shift in thinking led to other obvious changes in the way in which truth (if it existed at all) was viewed. Ideas have consequences. When we board an ideological train, we must take it all the way to its destination.

From Objective Authority to Relativism

When man uses his freedom to disregard God, he is on his own in the world. Yet he must face ultimate questions: What is the purpose of life? What is the highest good, and how can it be achieved? How can matters such as morality and values be found? Human reason, for all its potential, has severe limitations. Yes, man has made many scientific advances; we have put men on the moon and created complicated computers that can do wonders in a split second. We are indeed remarkably gifted.

But when it comes to matters of ultimate importance we simply find ourselves unable to make sense out of the reality around us. We can work with the observable world of nature and science, but when we speculate about that which lies beyond our senses, we grope for understanding. Scientific study can tell us how to make a bomb, but it cannot tell us if or how it should be used.

Since there is no way to measure morality and religion by our own speculations, man must opt for relativism, the view that there is no fixed reference point by which morality and religions can be judged. All cultures, and ultimately all lifestyles, must be private and largely beyond evaluation.

But can't we establish values on the basis of whatever promotes happiness or the general good of all? Plausible as this may seem, it is impossible. For one thing, there is no consensus on what is "best" for mankind; for another there can be no agreement as to how the "best" is to be achieved. Add to that the selfishness of the human heart, and we must confess that, left to ourselves, each of us does whatever "seems right in his own eyes," as the author of the book of Judges put it.

Our problem is that we are, in the words of William James, who should have taken himself more seriously when he said we are "like dogs in a library, seeing the books but unable to read the print." As victims of our own autonomous freedom, we have to make up our own meaning, seek our own happiness, and yet in the end see everything we have worked to achieve snatched from us in death. Little wonder some thoughtful people commit suicide!

This helps us understand why religion in America has been privatized. When the Bible was rejected the basis for moral and spiritual knowledge collapsed, and religion was reduced to a matter of personal opinion. Christ might be right for some people, Hinduism might be right for others. Or, preferably, a mixture of the two might be the best for someone else. You can create your own religious recipe suited to individual taste and preference. As Martin Marty has said, "People pick and choose truths as if on a cafeteria line, until they get the right mixture." At the end of the day, everybody is just as right as everybody else. And woe to the intolerant person who suggests that when beliefs conflict somebody must be wrong.

Woody Allen, who justified his sexual relationship with his stepdaughter, said, "The heart wants what it wants." As with morality, so it is in religion—you have yours, I have mine and there is no way for us to decide who is right. *Whatever my heart believes becomes right for me.*

From Objectivity to Pragmatism

If there is no fixed point of reference; if there is no objective basis for morality and religion, then we must accept relativism and its twin ideological brother, pragmatism: *Whatever works becomes right.*

William James wrote a book titled *Pragmatism* in which he says that "if the hypothesis of God works satisfactorily in the widest sense of the word, it is true."[6] He insisted that we must postpone our answer to the question of which religion is best because "we do not yet know certainly which religion is going to work best in the long run." We should judge all viewpoints by how much of a bang we get for our buck (he called it the "cash value" of a religious belief).

Michael Horton, in his excellent book *Made in America— The Shaping of Modern American Evangelicalism,* points out that today Christianity has to compete with a variety of self-help programs. It has to produce health, wealth, and happiness. Hypnotism, we are told, helps overcome smoking; pills can be taken to overcome obesity; and therapy helps those who are sexually addicted. Christianity is compared to a whole welter of self-help programs that are guaranteed to maximize the amount of happiness of individuals through financial and personal success. "Like a new bug spray," Horton writes, "God has to pass the test of utility for admission into the marketplace."[7]

But, Horton goes on to point out, the Bible was not written to compete with such pragmatic self-help techniques. "We must go back to the Scriptures for the questions as well as the answers," he says.[8] The Bible insists that the chief end of man is not to attain happiness, but rather to glorify God. It is the manner in which depraved sinners can be received by the Almighty. Christianity does promise deliverance from sin for those who are willing to come to Christ in repentance and faith, but it is not in tandem with the self-help craze. It's not just another in a series of books but one that sits on an entirely different shelf.

William James says we need a religion that works. Does Christianity work? Ask the martyrs who were not delivered from the lions whether their faith worked. Ask those who seek God for healing and yet die of a dehumanizing disease. Ask the man who became a Christian and his wife left him because she was antagonistic to his newfound faith. Based on our finite observations, Christianity doesn't always work.

Now, of course, if you ask whether Christianity works in reconciling us to God; if you ask whether it works in preparing us for death and the eternity that awaits us, then yes, we have good reason to believe it works very well. In fact, as the rest of this book will attempt to show, it is the only faith that works. But we cannot judge a belief purely on the basis of finite day-by-day observation. What appears to work today will not work tomorrow. What works for time might not work for eternity. Modern man might not be asking how he can be declared righteous by God so that he can enjoy heaven rather than suffer in hell, but that is precisely the question that Christianity claims to answer.

Horton correctly says that when Christianity is exploited for its usefulness, it becomes vulnerable to adaptation, amalgamation, and stagnation. If it is to remain as the "power of God unto salvation," it must not be judged by the immediate, superficial observation. It is concerned primarily with ultimate questions, not the question of how we can better our day-by-day existence.

From Reason to Feeling

A firm faith in God and belief in the Bible's authority have always led to the conviction that objective religious and moral truth can be discovered. The Puritans, like the sixteenth-century Reformers, believed that there should be no divorce between the heart and the mind. Their emotions were enlivened by great thoughts about God and His ways in the world. Puritan sermons combined theology, philosophy, and rational discourse based on the Bible as a way of looking at the world. They believed that a warm heart grows out of a full mind that worships an awesome God.

Theology was once considered the queen of the sciences, but in the absence of an authoritative source of knowledge, it has now become obsolete. The question for us moderns is not what religious ideas can be supported by rational data but what feels the best. Psychology has been substituted for theology. The serious pursuit of truth has been replaced by the pursuit of personal happiness. The Jewish philosopher Will Herberg said, "We are surrounded on all sides by the wreckage of our great intellectual tradition. . . . Instead of freedom we have the all-engulfing whirl of pleasure and power; instead of order, we have the jungle wilderness of normlessness and self-indulgence."[9]

Sin is no longer the great enemy of mankind; sadness is. To feel good about oneself is the number one priority. The Bible is reduced to a devotional guide to help people get in touch with their feelings. Thus Christianity is widely ignored in our culture despite the excellent evidence for its superiority among other alternatives. Our culture is not interested in serious arguments and rational evidence for matters of religion.

This undermining of the intellectual pursuit of truth, Horton points out, leaves Christianity without a serious defense in the marketplace of ideas, a marketplace from which it is now evicted. Some Christians, not to be outdone, have tried to argue that if you believe in Christ, you will feel better than you will with the alternatives. But the prospective convert asks: How do you know what will make me feel best? My feelings are my private property!

What happens when a generation accepts the idea that we should just feel, not think? People opt for opinions that fall short of convictions.

From Convictions to Opinions

Few people believe in anything anymore except, perhaps, the right to their own happiness. Understandably so, for if there is no objective truth, then nothing is worth dying for; and it follows that nothing is worth living for either.

Harvey Cox wrote,

Secularization has accomplished what fire and chain could not; it has convinced the believer that he could *be wrong,* and persuaded the devotee that there are more important things than dying for the faith. The gods of traditional religions live on as private fetishes or the patrons of congenial groups, but they play no role whatever in the public life of the secular metropolis.[10]

God has become a private fetish. His primary job description is to help us refurbish our deteriorating self-image. We have bought into those values of leisure, pleasure, and self-fulfillment that have made our God look compatible with our culture. This has forced us to retreat from the debate either for fear that the evidence for Christianity was too shaky or out of the perception that the basis of our faith is not important. In a world where feeling is the criterion of truth, we have closed both our minds and our mouths and pretended not to notice.

So how did we get here? When we rejected the Bible which is rooted in the soil of history and rational thought, we found that the only alternative was to reclassify religion and values as matters of personal opinion and private experiences. With the foundation gone the religious/moral house had to be moved to shifting sand where contradictions and absurdities had to somehow co-exist.

Or, to change the figure of speech, when the umpire's voice was drowned out by a chorus of competing voices, every player was free to write the rules to meet his own felt needs. Since everyone had a different opinion as to what was best for him, conflicting views had to be tolerated with no attempt to arbitrate between them. *Mindless tolerance became a pragmatic necessity.*

Mathematics, history, and science still held respect and thus were thought to be rational and objective. Religion and values, however, were put in a special file marked: *Private Opinions.* Truth was no longer thought to have any kind of universality but was simply a personal statement about what makes us feel good. Twenty-two thousand women met recently in Minneapolis for a conference under the banner of "Re-Imagining." The conference emphasized that women should create their own views of the deity from their own experiences. The goddess Sophia was honored, exemplifying that theology should be created "from the bottom up."

We are called to stand against our generation's insistence that religion does not deal with truth but is simply a matter of personal taste, such as whether one likes jazz or Bach. In the religious debate we must confront issues of truth. We have every right to ask for evidence when people make religious claims. We cannot let people feel comfortable with a faith that is equally at home with Christ and Shirley MacLaine. Private opinions must be exposed for what they are by pressing the question: "What evidence do you have that your views are true?"

We cannot concede the ideological war to a Babel of conflicting voices. We must redirect the focus of the battle to those issues that really matter. We can lovingly confront our generation with the Christ of the New Testament. We can show that evidence for His credibility is open for investigation. The roots of our faith can be laid bare for all to see.

YOUR RESPONSE TO THE MEGASHIFT

A man was driving past a farmyard when he noticed a sight that attracted his attention. On one side of the farmer's barn were numerous targets, and in the center of each one—right in the bull's eye—was an arrow. He was astonished to think that anyone could be such an expert marksman. He stopped his car to congratulate the farmer for his skill with the bow and arrow. The farmer was unimpressed, "This was not done by me," he explained, "it was done by the village idiot. He comes to my farm, shoots arrows into my barn, and paints the targets around them!"

If it is true, as Tozer has said, that what we believe about God is the most important thing about us, then we need to ask: What kind of a God has our society created? And to what extent have we modified our idea of God in light of cultural pressure? Listen to the media, our educators, and even our religious leaders and you get the impression that we are free to shoot the arrows wherever we wish and a benevolent God will approve every shot!

Radical feminism, homosexuality, a pinch of Eastern mysticism combined with a Western understanding of yoga, topped with verses of Scripture—all of this and more can be yours. Your god of choice will, of course, applaud your right to choose! There are no losers because God exists to make sure everyone hits the bull's eye!

Even we as evangelicals appear to have bowed to the tolerance of the age. Some have deleted the doctrine of eternal hell in favor of annihilationism, the view that the wicked are cast into hell and are totally consumed; others take the next step and teach that though Christ is the only way to God, personal faith in Him is not necessary for salvation. "My God," a man said to me with emphasis, "would never punish a single person!"

Harvey Cox argues that modern religion was born when we came to believe that God could be approached through "religious experiences" and thus "a faith which had once proclaimed a Lord who lifted up and cast down emperors, who condemned extortion and profit gouging, was now reduced to being concerned exclusively with the inner spirit or at most with friction between individuals." Cox quotes Nietzsche, who accused Christians of taming God, "You have caged [God], tamed him, domesticated him, and the priests have pliantly lent their aid. The roaring bull has become a listless ox. You have gelded God!"[11] We might say that the roaring bull has become a tolerant, listless ox.

So how do we topple this god named uncritical tolerance? First, we must press the claims of biblical Christianity. We must make the evidence for our faith available through our lives and words. We must encourage people to investigate Christ's claims and ask hard questions. In the end we must realize that the world does not need our ideas about God, but the world needs God's ideas about Himself and His relationship to us. And since there are good reasons to believe that He has revealed Himself in the Bible, we must point out why all other gods are idols.

Quite simply, we have a message that forces people to confront a God who has provided a way of redemption but who does not bend to social pressure nor mellow with age. The proclamation of a Christ who has the credentials to save is our only hope.

Karen Armstrong, who believes that the idea of God is a creation of the human mind, says, "Only western Christianity makes a song and dance about creeds and beliefs."[12] She insists that no twentieth-century Christian would "bother to start an argument about the divinity of Jesus . . . "

I invite you to join me as we *revive* that song and dance! Join me as we *stir up* some arguments about the divinity of Jesus! Let's *announce* that the shrine of uncritical tolerance cannot withstand scrutiny! *Let's draw a line and defend it!*

Ernst Renan, the French philosopher who lost his faith, wrote, "We are living on the perfume of an empty vase." Only an understanding of the uniqueness of Christ can refill that vase. We need a faith that reforms both the heart and the mind.

Second, if we wish to dethrone uncritical tolerance, we must understand what truth is. Before I present a portrait of Christ intended to show why He is the only reasonable option amid a blizzard of competing voices, we must answer the question Pilate asked Christ but left before he received the answer.

"What is truth?"

What do we say to those who believe that truth is personal and subjective? Why can't religion be privatized? What about the illustration of the wheel that says that we can be unified if we just move toward the hub? What are the characteristics of truth anyway?

Keep reading.

NOTES

1. Karen Armstrong, *A History of God* (New York: Random House, 1993). Quotes taken from *Time*, 27 September 1993, 77.
2. James Patterson and Peter Kim, *The Day America Told the Truth* (New York: Penguin Group, 1992), 201.

3. Allan Bloom, *The Closing of the American Mind* (New York: Simon and Schuster, 1987), 26.

4. Ibid., 64.

5. Joseph Haroutunian, *Piety Versus Moralism: The Passion of New England Theology* (New York: Harper and Sons, 1932), 145.

6. William James, *Pragmatism* (New York: Houghton Mifflin, 1955), 192.

7. Michael Scott Horton, *Made in America—The Shaping of Modern American Evangelicalism* (Grand Rapids: Baker, 1991), 49. This book has provided the stimulus for many of the ideas found in this chapter.

8. Ibid., 50.

9. Quoted in *Made in America,* 24.

10. Harvey Cox, *Religion in the Secular City: Toward a Postmodern Theology* (New York: Simon and Schuster, 1984), 200.

11. Ibid.

12. Armstrong, *A History*, quoted in *Time.*

THE
SEARCH
FOR TRUTH—

If It's True for Me, Is It True for You?

Let us use our imagination and join a small congregation on the outskirts of Rome in A.D. 303. The informal service has begun with prayer, the singing of hymns, and a number of laymen giving brief expositions from the Word. One speaker, the senior elder, has now taken the floor and is straining to speak. Obviously, it is difficult for him to form his words but he is determined, and so we listen.

He tells the congregation what they already suspected: The Emperor Diocletian has issued a new order, requiring all people to attend the religious/political ceremony designed to unify the nation and revive lagging patriotism within the empire. Specifically, this ceremony involves burning a bit of incense and saying simply "Caesar is Lord." Those who do this receive a seal of approval; those who don't might well be put to death.

After the speech, the believers ask questions and discuss what their response should be. The answer is not as obvious as it seems. For one thing, they actually would not have to stop worshiping the true God; after they have sworn their allegiance to Caesar as Lord, they are free to privately worship whatever god they wish. Every religion is tolerated; freedom to choose one's own god is generally accepted. Indeed, there is richness in diversity.

Second, this was not simply a religious decision, but a political one. Caesar was convinced that it was not possible to be a good citizen without affirming his lordship. The argument was that if one had allegiance to a god above Caesar he could not be trusted in a time of national emergency, a war, for instance. All good citizens were willing to "worship the spirit of Rome and the genius of the Emperor" as the edict read.

Third, this requirement was but once a year. Even if one did tell a lie, forgiveness through Christ was readily available. Why not argue, as some did, "For a moment my mouth belongs to the Emperor, though my heart always belongs to Christ."

Rome was cruel. Many converted pagans who were now in the church had observed firsthand the brutality of the Roman citizens. They had sat high above the arena floor in the Coliseum and had watched the gladiators combat; they had at one time cheered as Christians were thrown to the wild beasts. They had seen believers cry to God for deliverance, but nevertheless be torn to ribbons to the cheers of the bloodthirsty throngs.

If Christ were seen as one option among many, Christians could give allegiance to other expressions of the divine. Why not find common ground, the central unity of all religions? This would not only promote harmony but also the common good of the state. So the choice, strictly speaking, was not whether the Christians would worship Christ or Caesar; it was whether they would worship Christ *and* Caesar.

Interestingly, the pagans of the day saw no conflict between emperor worship and the worship of their own gods. In fact the Romans appeased their conquered nations by building the Pantheon, a beautiful temple in which all the gods and goddesses of the conquered peoples were displayed. Every god, they believed, represented the mystery of divinity. Why be locked into one expression of transcendence when it appears as if all the religions are saying the same thing? As we shall see, paganism both ancient and modern has always been tolerant of other finite gods.

As the elder speaks to the small gathering, little children with sad faces clutch the arms of their mothers. If their parents were to spurn the emperor and die, who would care for them? Might not it be best to make the political confession and be allowed to live for the benefit of the little ones? The elder urges believers to remain true to the faith, but he is aware that some will give Caesar what he demands. They claim to have discovered that there is more common ground between the faiths of Rome and Christianity than originally thought.

What would *you* do? What would *I* do? We cannot stand in judgment on those who worshiped Caesar, for we do not know what we would have done when faced with a similar choice. But most Christians—bless them—refused to believe that Christ could sit on the same shelf as the pagan gods. That is why the Christians did not want Rome to create a niche for Jesus in their pluralistic Pantheon. To understand Christ was to see Him so unique, so special, that divided loyalties could not exist in an honest heart even if just for a moment.

Official Rome abhorred such exclusivism, the idea that Christ was the only way to God. They believed that the Christians were unpatriotic (read "politically incorrect") to oppose the official gods who apparently did not mind competition. Rome also had other complaints about the Christians. Rumors circulated about their cannibalism (did they not claim to eat the flesh of Christ and drink His blood?). But for the most part, tolerance was the name of game—tolerance for those who displayed tolerance! But the lions awaited those who would not compromise their beliefs.

Our choice today is more subtle but in principle the same as that which the early Christians faced. True, we do not have to worship Caesar, though many would have us believe that there is no authority beyond the state. Nor do we have to fear that our lives are in jeopardy if we are committed to the Christian faith. But the temptation is there—the temptation to divide our loyalties, to crown Christ Lord but then give lesser crowns to competing loyalties.

We can see this most clearly in the person who claims to be a "Christian Buddhist" or the Sunday school teacher who combines Christianity with Yoga or other New Age beliefs. But such mixed allegiances are also tolerated when Christianity is combined with secular psychology or the growing notion that the problem of evil can be solved by believing in a finite God. We also see it in the person who compromises his or her integrity to keep a job. The temptation to idolatry, the powerful urge to combine Christ with other rivals, is ever with us. We are always tempted to be more tolerant than God.

The purpose of this chapter is to topple the idol of uncritical tolerance by showing:

1. That it is logically absurd to believe that all the religions of the world could be equally right

2. That truth has certain characteristics that are transcultural; privatized religion is a contradiction in terms

3. That we, individually, must come to the assurance that religious truth is objective, applicable to everyone

There is a story about a man who looked for his lost key under a street lamp even though he had dropped it farther up the road. When asked why he didn't search where he dropped it, he said he wanted to be where he could see! We are all like that. We all look at life through the light that is familiar to us. But when we seek the truth, we must be willing to move out of areas that are familiar to us and follow our search wherever it leads.

Don't skim this chapter! Join me as we take a brief tour of some of the major religions of the world to illustrate why they cannot all be equally true. Since there appear to be some similarities, we have to find out whether their differences are significant. Then we'll examine the popular notion that says, "Christ might be true for you but not for me." Does a belief *become* true if we just hold it with sincerity?

THE RELIGIONS OF THE WORLD CONFLICT

Edward Gibbon in *The Decline and Fall of the Roman Empire* stated that during the decline of the Roman Empire, all religions were regarded by the people as *equally true,* by the philosophers as *equally false,* and by the politicians as *equally useful!*

Could the people have been right? Could all the religions of the world be equally true? Philosopher John Hick in his book *The Myth of Christian Uniqueness*[1] argues that Christianity has nothing special to commend it; if unity is to be achieved, we must surrender the idea that one religion should be preferred above another. In fact, one of the contributors to the book, Wilfred Kantwell Smith, says there is no such thing as idolatry. All religions have as their common core some experience of the transcendent, whether of wood or stone or even our reflection of Jesus Himself. Since God accepts all worship, the claim to uniqueness is blasphemous!

I hope that by the time you have finished reading this chapter, you will agree that this point of view is both illogical and preposterous. Worse, it leads to frightening conclusions.

Ravi Zacharias has observed that most people think all the religions of the world are essentially the same and only superficially different. But the opposite, he says, is the case: The religions of the world are essentially different and only superficially the same.

Let's quickly compare a few major religions in only two doctrines: (1) their understanding of God, or the Religious Ultimate; and (2) their doctrine of salvation.

The Religious Ultimate

As you might have guessed, the major non-Christian religions not only disagree regarding their understanding of the Religious Ultimate, or God, but they don't even agree on whether such a being (of whatever description) exists!

Hinduism believes in 300,000 gods. Most devotees revere or worship a few favorites but respect them all. If we ask how these gods can peacefully co-exist, the answer is that they only represent an impersonal force, Brahman, the One, the Soul of the Cosmos. Our goal is to lose our identity in this ultimate Oneness.

Hinduism is not concerned with contradictions, hence there are many and often conflicting paths to the same Ultimate Reality. Logic, it is said, exists on a lower plane. As we approach the

Ultimate, all distinctions vanish and everything converges into the One. Like the other Eastern religions, Hinduism is best described as a tree with many different and conflicting branches. Since it has absorbed many pagan ideas, it does not have a body of clearly-defined doctrines.

The Shinto religion, found primarily in Japan, is animistic, believing that gods (kami) reside in all creatures—even trees, the soil, or objects. But let us not think of these gods as distinct from the objects they inhabit; they are a part of the natural world. These gods are indifferent to morality and make no contribution to the battle between good and evil. Since the gods are seldom offended, sin does not exist. Disharmony, yes; sin, no.

In contrast, most Buddhists do not even believe in a god (or gods). When the Parliament of the World's Religions issued a Global Ethic, it did not even use the word *God* because some Buddhists would have been offended. The monks insisted that when a Buddhist prays, he is actually meditating, speaking only to himself.

Islam is monotheistic (affirms belief in one God), a concept which was borrowed from the Hebrew-Christian tradition. This deity is not a trinity, and he is so far removed from us that he could never become man. Allah is not the God and Father of our Lord Jesus Christ but actually was the tribal deity of Mohammed, who elevated his god to the position of Supreme Ruler.[2] Nor can Allah be associated with other non-Christian gods because of the basic creed, "There is no god but Allah and Mohammed is his prophet." His moral and spiritual distance from us makes it necessary that He be largely removed from the events of this world. Fatalism, often a cruel fatalism, rules.

The bottom line: The non-Christian religions cannot even agree on a basic understanding of the Religious Ultimate. Think of how vast the differences would be if we compared these ideas with Christianity!

The Doctrine of Salvation

Hindus and Buddhists believe that we are trapped in a cycle of rebirths; we transmigrate, though how we do so is unclear. Both religions believe man's problem is not sin but ignorance. Through meditation and obedience we can be brought from confusion to reality.

But at this point, the two religions part ways: Buddhists are committed to the eight paths of Buddha, hope for Nirvana which is the elimination of all desire. Hindus, in turn, seek freedom from karma through disinterested selfless action. Shintos have no clear doctrine of the afterlife and therefore believe that salvation is striving to have a healthy, robust life in the here and now.

In Islam salvation comes by doing the will of Allah which is spelled out in "the five pillars." In the day of judgment some will be consigned to hell and others to a paradise filled with sensual delights. Worshipers of gods other than Allah will certainly go to hell; but no one, not even a devoted Muslim, can know his eternal fate with certainty. One can only hope that in the day of judgment the good will outweigh the bad.

If we had the time to explore these religions in more detail, we would discover that different answers are given to the most basic questions. Is there one God or many? Is he/Are they personal or non-personal? Is our problem sin or ignorance? Is salvation simply living a healthy life or restoration to a God or gods? Or is it release from a cycle of rebirths? If there is a heaven or a hell, what are they like?

For now, it is enough to realize that if all the religions of the world were equally true the universe would be a cosmic madhouse! To put it differently, if all the religions of the world are equally true, logic requires that they all are equally false: *The conflicting doctrines would cancel one another!*

Don't accept the idea that these logical differences are important only to Westerners. The Eastern religions claim that contradictions can exist side by side. Truth, it is said, is not a matter of either/or but is a synthesis of both/and. Thus contradictions can be left unresolved. But those who are critical of logic use logic in a vain attempt to get their point across.

You might remember that in *Alice in Wonderland,* Alice was able to believe as many as six contradictions before breakfast. But anyone who can believe two contradictions before lunch, must, I am sorry to say, be declared insane! Let me say emphatically that the laws of logic are transcultural; they apply just as much to the Hindu as they do to the Muslim; they apply just as much to the Buddhist as they do to the Christian. Logically, all the religions of the world may be false, but they cannot all be true.

Example: We simply cannot believe that there is only one God (Christianity) and yet there are also 300,000 valid gods (Hinduism). We can't believe that Nirvana, heaven, paradise, hell, freedom from karma, and losing one's identity in an impersonal ultimate are all compatible doctrines. As C. S. Lewis said, "Those who call for nonsense will find that it comes."

Think this through: If the laws of logic are invalid, no Easterner can criticize me for believing the opposite of what he believes. He can believe that truth is both/and, a synthesis of two conflicting doctrines. But I can believe that truth is either/or, namely that truth must follow the strict laws of logic. Though our views conflict, this should be of no concern since the Easterner believes that contradictions exist side by side. Even if I believe he is wholly in error, he cannot dispute my conclusions. After all, unless truth is consistent and logical, one can always believe the opposite of what another believes. In such a world, absurdity is king!

The Bible is very clear that no contradictions can exist. The presence of truth means that the opposite is error.

> Do not be bound together with unbelievers; for what partnership have righteousness and lawlessness, or what fellowship has light with darkness? Or what harmony has Christ with Belial, or what has a believer in common with an unbeliever? Or what agreement has the temple of God with idols? For we are the temple of the living God. (2 Corinthians 6:14–16)

All the religions of the world cannot be equally true. Choose we must, for the dissimilarities are as profound as light and darkness, God and Satan, heaven and hell. Doctrinal distinctions are important, often contradictory, and logically necessary.

ALL RELIGIONS CLAIM TO BE TRUE

If the religions of the world conflict with one another, how can unity be achieved? Obviously each religion would have to surrender its claim to truth and only speak of having a different perspective of the truth. But the problem is that even these "perspectives" are in sharp conflict. Philosophers might ask us to give up any notion of truth, but this is impossible without destroying the essence of religion.

As every religious person knows, Hindus believe in karma and reincarnation because they think these doctrines actually correspond to the way things are (they believe them to be true). Christians believe in the Trinity and strongly disagree with Islam which denies the deity of Christ and holds that Mohammed was a prophet of God. Would any one of the followers of these religions be willing to say, "I believe these doctrines, but I do not claim they are true"? I think not.

If the religions of the world would surrender their claim to truth, no Hindu could ever give evidence for karma, no Buddhist would disagree with Christians who believe in a personal God. Religion would be nothing but a matter of cultural or personal preference. Can you imagine everyone agreeing in advance that to discuss religion is to discuss error because no religion claims it has the truth?

We can avoid this impasse, some say, by stripping our doctrines of any literal significance and seeking a hidden symbolic meaning. During an evening performance at the Parliament of the World's Religions, a voice came over the sound system, "We are building a sacred place that will hold all our polarities and our paradoxes." In other words, the goal was to construct a religious edifice flexible enough to house all the world's faiths under one spiritual roof. If we weren't so narrow-minded and were all willing to give a little bit, maybe it could be done.

Let's find out why such a goal is not logically possible. Truth cannot be bent to accommodate the religions of the world. Which leads me to the question: What is truth anyway?

CHARACTERISTICS OF TRUTH

"If you abide in My word, then you are truly disciples of Mine; and you shall know the truth and the truth shall make you free" Christ told His disciples (John 8:31–32). Whether we accept Christ's authority or not, we do have to agree that truth has certain necessary characteristics.

Truth Is Universal

When Christ claimed that truth exists, of necessity He also implied that falsehood exists. Your personal opinions about religion may be true; but if so, they are also true for everyone else. If you meet a friend who says, "Christ is true for you, but not for me," tell him lovingly, "You are entitled to your own private *opinion*, but you are not entitled to your own private *truth!*"

Mathematics is transcultural; it is foolish to say that $2 + 2 = 4$ is simply a Western idea. Science and technology also rely on universal principles that apply in every country, in every era. When an astronomer finds a new star, he has not changed the nature of the universe; he has only found something that was already there. *Truth exists objectively outside ourselves*. We do not create it; we can only discover it.

Does this objectivity also apply to religion, or is religion purely personal and subjective? Logic requires that if there is one God then there are not two, three, or ten. If what Christ said was true, then what Bahá ú lláh said was false. You may live next door to a fine Mormon family, but Mormonism and Christianity cannot both be true. Both may be false, but both cannot be true. And if one religion of the world is objectively true, it is true for everyone. The issue is *whether we have committed ourselves to a religion that reflects the way things are in the universe.*

We must resist the modern notion that there is a sharp distinction between the world of objective facts (mathematics, science, etc.) and the realm of religion, which many believe should be relegated to the private world of personal opinion and individual preferences. Religion, if it is worth the name, claims to make factual statements about spiritual reality. This means that every religion has the responsibility of giving evidence for its truth claims. Such evidence should be accessible to believers and nonbelievers alike.

Christ presented Himself as the one and only qualified Savior who is able to bring men and women to God the Father (reasons for this will be given in subsequent chapters). Logically, this excludes all other teachers/gurus who claim that they can bring men and women to God. Nor can Christ be the Savior for only the Western world, but not the Eastern world. If He is the truth, He is the truth for everyone. Whether one accepts Christ or not is a separate question, but He is either the truth for all or the truth for none.

The superscription nailed above the cross is not a *proof* of Christ's universality, but it is a striking *illustration* of it. Though Pilate had the caption written in three languages for the benefit of the visitors in Jerusalem during the Passover, it fits with Christ's own claims to be the Lord, the King. The custom was to place a placard above the head of a criminal so passersby could see what crime led to the execution. The words above Christ's head read, *"This is the king of the Jews."* We read, "Therefore this inscription many of the Jews read, for the place where Jesus was crucified was near the city; and it was written in Hebrew, Latin, and in Greek" (John 19:20). These were the three most important languages of the ancient world.

It was written in Hebrew. This was the language of religion. Throughout the centuries God revealed Himself through this beautiful language. Abraham was called the Hebrew; the prophets spoke in the same tongue. This was the language that carried that weight of revelation. Christ had claimed the realm of religion for His own.

Latin was the language of government. From the splendor of the seven hills of Rome, the caesars prided themselves in ruling the whole earth. They built great roads and established trade to the farthest part of the then-known world. Their goal was to plant the Roman flag on every shore. The language that carried their legal system, the language in which the world was trained to think about government and commerce was Latin. Christ claimed that eventually He would rule the world (Matthew 25:31).

Then there was Greek, the language of culture. The Greeks could take clay and stone and from them create items of beauty. The perfection of their sculptures is still unrivaled. In philosophy they gave us Plato, Socrates, and Aristotle whose teachings have intrigued the world. And when Alexander the Great set out on his conquests, he said that he hoped to make all the world Greek. Christ, as will become clear, claimed to be greater than the honored cultural men of His day.

When Christ said, "I am the way, and the truth, and the life; no one comes to the Father, but through Me" (John 14:6), it seems clear that He did not think of Himself as the truth for some people, but not others. Again, He said, "And I, if I be lifted up from the earth, will draw all men to Myself" (John 12:32). Whether we find truth in science, history, mathematics, or religion, it has objectivity and universality.

Let those who reject Christ do so, but let them realize that if He is not the truth for them, He is not the truth for His followers either. If He is the only qualified Savior of the world as He claimed, all others are excluded. If He is only the Savior for some, His claims are false and He is not a Savior for any.

"The truth," says Carl F. Henry, "is not subject to revision as are the airline schedules . . . the good and the true cannot be reduced to whatever Hollywood and Madison Avenue momentarily approve, or to whatever culture-ridden sociologists and secular humanists commend."[3] We may disagree regarding what is truth and what is error, but let us never think that both do not exist.

Truth Is Consistent

Christianity asserts that not even God is capable of self-contradictions. He cannot both deny and affirm the same thing in the same way and at the same time. If He could, not a single one of His promises could be trusted, for its opposite might be equally true!

So what do we say to those ecumenically-minded folks who tell us that we must discard our differences and unite on the basis of inner experience? Think back to the wheel (described in chapter 1) that supposedly illustrates that as the different religions (spokes) move toward the hub they become unified. Think with me to see if this illustration is helpful or misleading.

First, it assumes that truth and error can do what the spokes of a wheel can do. Certainly spokes can be laid in such a way that they converge in the center. But if the spokes accurately represented truth and error, they would have to lie parallel to each other. They would be like railway tracks which run parallel and would do so throughout all of eternity. Even in eternity, two plus two will never become five. Error never becomes truth, and truth does not become error.

Second, this illustration gives the impression that when leaving the rim (doctrine) and moving toward the center, nothing important is lost in the process. Doctrine, we are told, is the least important aspect of religion and therefore can be compromised or reinterpreted in varying degrees. But is not the outer part of the rim the most important? Does not what is in the outer rim (doctrine) determine what we experience in the hub?

To illustrate: I've pointed out that Christianity asserts that God has provided only one Savior for the world, namely, Jesus Christ. Another Christian doctrine is that Satan exists and can give misleading experiences to those who try to approach God through some other teacher, technique, or doctrine. Think of these doctrines as being at the rim of the wheel. Can we discard them and move toward the hub in the interest of unity? No. Because *what we experience at the hub is determined by what we believe at the rim!*

At the Parliament of the World's Religions, I was surprised by the number of people who agreed with me when I shared my belief that Satan is often encountered in transcendental meditation. Some answered, "Yes, we encounter evil, but we have to go through it to get to the other side." Others admitted that yes, they were acquainted with the power of Satan and needed a guru to help purify them through the encounter. What interesting encounters take place in that religious "hub" of the wheel!

As Christians, we interpret the "hub" by the "rim." We believe that Satan is delighted when people experience him and think they are encountering "the Religious Ultimate" or God (of whatever variety). When warning against false teachers, Paul says that they will disguise themselves as apostles of Christ, "And no wonder, for even Satan disguises himself as an angel of light" (2 Corinthians 11:14). Christianity insists that all experience must be based on correct doctrine. No sensible Christian will discard his fundamental beliefs for the sake of an undefined and possibly deceptive experience. *Right doctrine produces valid experiences; false doctrine produces deceptive ones.*

What happens when religion is reclassified as nothing more than personal opinion? Modern man no longer has a criterion by which competing ideas about God can be judged. As Lesslie Newbigin has pointed out, Hitler was certain that he had a mission from God. Do we take his word for it? If not, on what grounds do we deny his testimony?[4] Without an objective standard, everyone is free to affirm even a demonic god, and we have no rational reason to say he is wrong. In a world of uncritical pluralism, in a world where idolatry is impossible, each person's idea of God or gods has just as much validity as that of someone else. Thankfully, Christ has the qualifications to arbitrate among conflicting perspectives.

But what do we say to the person who says, "I'm into Eastern mysticism, and *it works* for me!" We must remind him that there is a difference between the question, "What works?" and, "What is true?" We all know that error can "work" (we're reminded of the Sunday school boy who said, "A lie is an abomination to the Lord but a very present help in trouble!"). Yes, a lie can work. But when error works, it does so only for a limited time and for a limited purpose. No error can work indefinitely. Only truth endures in this life and the life to come.

Truth Can Be Known

Even skeptics must ruefully admit that at least some truth can be known. Even the denial that truth can be found is itself an assertion of "truth." Skeptics who disdain religious ideas believe that their insights should be regarded as "true." There are no genuine skeptics.

Christ said, "Ye shall know the truth and the truth shall set you free." He affirmed that truth can be known. This is not to say that we can know religious truth exhaustively, for we are limited in understanding ourselves and our relationship with God. We see through a glass darkly, but we do see.

Because Christianity is a revelation from God, it asserts that we not only have truth but it has come to us in a form that we can understand. The search for truth is not hopeless. To love God is to love truth.

Truth Brings Freedom

Skeptics agree that we spend our lives seeking truth. We may want to find the truth about our coworker, about our neighbors, and about our spouse. Communication assumes that there is truth and error; it also assumes that truth is preferable to error, and knowing the difference is important for our well-being.

The same can be said for religious truth. If it exists and can be known, it would unlock many mysteries that plague the mind. How did we get here? What is the purpose of our existence? What will happen in the future? How can we find fulfillment? Truth has power; it can be liberating.

When Christ said that truth brings freedom, He was speaking of a certain kind of freedom, a freedom that many people might not care to have, but a freedom that at least some would seek. The Jews did not see themselves as having been slaves to anyone, therefore they were puzzled by Christ's words. But Christ was not speaking about political or economic freedom. He was speaking of spiritual freedom, the privilege of being free from the tyranny of sin. In the end that kind of freedom, He taught, is the most important of all.

Truth Should Be Prized

Why did the Christians say no when the Romans were willing to create a niche for Jesus in the Pantheon? They understood two premises: First, *there is an unbridgeable gap between the infinite, personal God and all finite gods.* Since there is good evidence that finite gods are the creation of men, it is understandable that such gods are indifferent to competition! One finite god must make room for another. Finite gods can harmonize their diverse and conflicting attributes because individually they make no claim to objective truth. Thus, the New Age movement can afford to promote a tolerance of sorts, a tolerance for any number of finite gods. So can the ecumenical movement, or the Parliament of the World's Religions.

But in the presence of the infinite, personal God all other gods must vanish, "For the Lord is a great God, And a great King above all gods" (Psalm 95:3). This God is rightly jealous for His own honor and therefore proclaims in the first commandment, "You shall have no other gods before Me" (Exodus 20:3). Finite gods must tolerate one another; but confronted by the Almighty, they must capitulate and thus prove they are really not gods at all.

Second, the early Christians understood that *Christ was not simply a prophet, guru, or religious leader.* They believed Him to be a Savior, One who had come down from heaven, not just to instruct us but to lift us out of our sins. They saw Him to be the One true God, manifest in the flesh. They saw Caesar crushed beneath His feet. How then could they give ultimate loyalty to a mere man when they had pledged ultimate loyalty to the God/man?

They saw an unbridgeable chasm between Christianity and all other options. They believed that to search for religious truth elsewhere was to lead to a dead end. Any similarities between their religion and the religions of Rome were superficial and misleading. They were committed to truth, its universality and consistency. They would have agreed with Bishop Neill, "If Christianity is purged of its uniqueness it is transformed into something other than itself; it's like taking chlorine from hydrochloride."

When we minimize the difference between Christianity and other religions, we miss the central core of its teachings. The rest of this book is dedicated to showing that Christ stands alone, unrivaled, and ultimately unopposed.

Join me as we seek Him out.

NOTES

1. John Hick and Paul F. Knitter, eds. *The Myth of Christian Uniqueness: Toward a Pluralistic Theology of Religions* (Mary Knoll, N.Y.: Orbis Books, 1987).
2. Robert A. Morey, *Islam Unveiled* (Shermans, Pa.: The Scholars Press, 1991), 46–51.
3. Carl F. Henry, *Christian Countermoves in a Decadent Culture* (Portland: Multnomah, 1986), 110.
4. Lesslie Newbigin, "Religious Pluralism and the Uniqueness of Jesus Christ," *International Bulletin of Missionary Research,* April 1989, 50.

AN
EXTRAORDINARY
BIRTH—

What Does It Take to Be a Savior?

You probably saw this heartbreaking story in your local newspaper: A grandmother was taking care of her two-year-old granddaughter when the little girl fell into the swimming pool. Although the woman did not know how to swim, she hopped into the water in a desperate effort to rescue the child. Hours later both bodies were found at the bottom of the pool.

When you're drowning, you need help from someone who meets two requirements: First he must be *willing* to rescue you, but that in itself will not do; second, the person must be *able* to rescue you. You will not be brought to the shore successfully by someone who is himself going under. Only a person who has mastered the water, a person who is in control of his immediate surroundings, can become a savior. A rescuer cannot be a person who himself needs to be rescued!

The Bible teaches and our experience confirms that we are sinners, and, as a race, separated from God. Our own efforts at self-transformation might improve our lifestyle or even our attitude, but fundamentally we are left unchanged. Our greatest need is to be forgiven, reconciled to God and rescued from the present tyranny and future consequences of our sin. For that, we need a Savior.

At this point Christianity and all other religions part ways.

Every religion has its prophets, its teachers or gurus who tell us how we can better ourselves, how we can become our own savior of sorts. In effect they tell us we are drowning, but they will help us make our descent to the bottom of the ocean more comfortable. Or they might even claim to give us swimming lessons. But only a Savior—a qualified Savior—can reach out to snatch us from the power of the undercurrent.

Christ and only Christ claims to be able to give us a sturdy hand. He does not bark out orders telling us that if we swim harder we might live a few minutes longer. He does not hold out a limp hand saying, "I'm a fellow struggler just like you; let's join hands and go to the bottom together." Nor does He point to the shore and leave the rest up to us. He knows, even if we do not, that our predicament is serious, our attempt to rectify our relationship with God, impossible. The purpose of Christ's coming was stated before His birth when the angel said to Joseph, "And she will bear a Son; and you shall call His name Jesus, for it is He who will save His people from their sins" (Matthew 1:21). Years later He stated his own job description, "For the Son of Man has come to seek and to save that which was lost" (Luke 19:10).

Of course there have always been those who have wanted to strip Him of his qualifications. Liberal scholars and media gurus have often insisted that Christ was Himself drowning, just as we are. When Martin Scorsese directed the film, "The Last Temptation of Christ," he said, "I tried to create a Jesus, who in a sense, is just like any other guy in the street." When he was finished he had a Christ who was not even a prophet, much less a Savior. This Christ was not even worthy of respect, much less worship.

When I look into my own heart, when I am aware of my sinfulness and God's holiness, I need something more than another "guy on the street" who is as sinful as I am. I don't need lessons in swimming; I need someone to pick me up, cleanse me, and take me to God.

IN SEARCH OF A SINLESS SAVIOR

At the Parliament of the World's Religions, I walked through the display area in search of a sinless prophet/teacher/

Savior. I asked a Hindu Swami whether any of their teachers claimed sinlessness. "No" he said, appearing irritated with my question, "if anyone claims he is sinless, he is not a Hindu!"

What about Buddha? No, I was told, he didn't claim sinlessness. He found a group of ascetics and preached sermons to them. He taught that all outward things are only distractions and encouraged a life of discipline and contemplation. He sought enlightenment and urged his followers to do the same. He died seeking enlightenment. No sinlessness here.

What about Bahá ú lláh? He claimed he had a revelation from God that was more complete, more enlightened than those before him. Though he was convinced of the truth of his teachings, he made few personal claims. He thought his writings were "more perfect" than others, but he never claimed perfection or sinlessness for himself.

When I came to the representatives of the Muslim faith, I already knew that in the Koran the prophet Mohammed admitted he was in need or forgiveness. They agreed. "There is one God, Allah and Mohammed is His prophet" is the basic Muslim creed. But Mohammed was not perfect. Again, no sinlessness there.

Why was I searching for a sinless Savior? Because I don't want to have to trust a Savior who is in the same predicament as I am. I can't trust my eternal soul to someone who is still working through his own imperfections. Since I'm a sinner, I need someone who is standing on higher ground.

Understandably, none of the religious leaders I spoke with even claimed to have a Savior. Their prophets, they said, showed the way but made no pretense to be able to personally forgive sins or transform so much as a single human being. Like a street sign, they gave directions but were not able to take us where we need to go; if we need any saving, we will have to do it ourselves. The reason is obvious: No matter how wise, no matter how gifted, no matter how influential other prophets, gurus, and teachers might be, they had the presence of mind to know that they were imperfect just like the rest of us. They never even presumed to be able to reach down into the murky water of human depravity and bring sinners into the presence of God.

How different was Christ!

"Which one of you convicts Me of sin? If I speak truth, why do you not believe Me?" (John 8:46). He pointed out hypocrisy in the lives of His critics, but none of them returned the compliment.

Judas, an apparent friend turned enemy, said, "I have sinned by betraying innocent blood" (Matthew 27:4).

Pilate, who longed to find fault with Christ, confessed, "I find no guilt in this man" (Luke 23:4).

Peter, who lived with Him for three years, said He "committed no sin, nor was any deceit found in His mouth" (1 Peter 2:22).

The apostle Paul said that God the Father "made Him who knew no sin to be sin on our behalf, that we might become the righteousness of God in Him" (2 Corinthians 5:21).

Jesus was either sinless or the greatest of sinners for deceiving so many people about His sinlessness. As C. E. Jefferson puts it, "The best reason we have for believing in the sinlessness of Jesus is the fact that he allowed his dearest friends to think that he was."

Why was Christ exempt from the sin with which we are so well acquainted? If He, like us, would have had a human father, He would have had a sin nature that is passed on from father to son. If He had been the son of Adam in a natural way, He would have been a sinner.

The virgin conception preserved His sinlessness. Mary experienced a special miracle that ensured the perfection of her son. He was like us but with an important difference.

THE NECESSITY OF THE VIRGIN BIRTH

To be a Savior, Christ had to meet three requirements. First, he had to be a male, born of a woman as predicted in Genesis 3:15. He had to become one of us to redeem us. No angel could have borne our sin; He had to represent us in all respects.

Second, He had to be sinless in order to have the perfection God demands. As sinners, we cannot pay for our own sin even if we suffered forever, much less could we pay for the sin of someone else. Whether the sacrifice was accepted depended on its value, its perfection.

Third, He also had to be God, so that it could be said that God Himself undertook a rescue mission to reconcile sinful humanity. If salvation is of the Lord, He had to provide the very sacrifice He demanded.

Let's review this bit of theology: When Adam sinned, the whole human race was involved. Just like the mighty oak tree is in the acorn, so all of us were in Adam and we inherited his sinfulness. Paul made it clear that we not only all sinned in Adam, but through him we are sinners by nature. If Christ was to be sinless, He could not have a human father.

But might not Christ have been born as an ordinary child, and then at a later time (perhaps at His baptism) been infused with the divine nature? That's been suggested, but this theory poses another problem, namely, What would have happened to the sins He had committed prior to this transformation? Christ didn't become someone different; He was the same person He always was.

Others have argued that if Christ had had a human father, God still could have done a miracle and made Him sinless. Since God is capable of all kinds of miracles, that is possible, but as Alva J. McClain wrote, "A sinless man in the moral realm would be a greater miracle than the virgin birth in the biological realm."

Notice how plainly the virgin conception is taught, "Now the birth of Jesus Christ was as follows. When His mother Mary had been betrothed to Joseph, before they came together she was found to be with child by the Holy Spirit" (Matthew 1:18).

Luke records, "And Mary said to the angel, 'How can this be, since I am a virgin?' And the angel answered and said to her, 'The Holy Spirit will come upon you, and the power of the Most High will overshadow you; and for that reason the holy offspring shall be called the Son of God'" (1:34, 35). The unborn child was already holy!

God, I'm sure, could have preserved Christ's sinlessness in different ways, but He chose to accomplish this through a virgin conception. The fetus is described as a "holy offspring," words that cannot apply to any one of us. Like us He was conceived in a woman, but He was without sin. The incarnation already took place in the womb of Mary.

As we might expect, there have always been those who have denied the virgin birth. They are determined to strip Christ of His credentials to be a Savior; they insist that He was only a man, capable of pointing us toward ethical ideals but no more qualified than we in lifting us out of our own sinfulness. He is perhaps even able to give us "swimming lessons," but He is unable to extend a powerful hand.

Maybe you have struggled with your belief in the virgin birth. You may have heard that it is based on ancient mythologies found in other religions and diverse pagan legends. Let's survey some of the objections and see whether they make sense.

OBJECTIONS TO THE VIRGIN BIRTH

Opposition to this doctrine began early in the history of the church and continues today.

The Accounts Were Borrowed from Mythology

Great people always had a supernatural birth attributed to them. For example, Zeus, it was said, was father of the gods and men; he is represented as begetting children with human mothers. Diana was beloved of Zeus and conceived a child by a shower of gold which descended upon her in seclusion; as a result Perseus was born. Hercules was also the child of Zeus, who impregnated a mortal woman. There was a rumor that Plato was fathered by the god Apollo.

There is a myth that Alexander the Great also had an unusual birth. When his mother's marriage was consummated, there was a clap of thunder and lightning struck her womb. Her husband Philip was required to seal up her womb, and she conceived and bore Alexander. Another legend says that Alexander's mother conceived after swallowing a pomegranate.

Could pagan mythology have inspired Matthew and Luke

to tell a tale about the miraculous conception of Jesus? Did these authors have a reason to attribute such stories to Christ? Don't answer until you think it through.

These legends grew out of pagan polytheism, the belief that there are many gods who were powerful men with human lusts, jealousies, and hates; the context was sexuality and fertility. In mythology, the gods enjoyed human sexual pleasures; in fact, when the orgies were finished, the women could no longer be classified as virgins.

Is it feasible that the church would have borrowed ideas from pagan mythology at its most degrading point? Would the writers have incorporated the polytheistic notions of pagans whom they perceived as enemies of the Jewish/Christian teachings? Matthew and Luke would never have written their narratives to show that Christ was just like other pagan heroes!

The thought that God found Mary sexually desirable is reprehensible and contrary to the whole spirit of the gospel writers. These narratives are, to quote the words of Robert Gromacki, "bathed in holiness." There is a moral and ethical gulf that separates the New Testament accounts from pagan mythology.

In contrast to these legends, the New Testament writers were sober and restrained and clearly intended that they be taken literally. The birth narratives are understated and have dignity, plausibility, and a high moral character.

It's worth noting that the pagan rumors about the gods impregnating women arose after individuals became famous. There are no documents that purport to have claimed such miracles at the time of the birth itself. In contrast, Christ's virgin conception was predicted.

The Accounts Came from Jewish Sources

Some have thought that the virgin birth was invented to preserve the reputation of Mary. The argument is that she became pregnant, either with Joseph or a man who claimed to be a messenger of God. To cover Mary's immoral relationship, she and her friends circulated a story about the virgin birth.

Or there are those who say that it was invented to fulfill prophecy. The Jews, the argument goes, based on Isaiah 7:14 were expecting the Messiah to be born of a virgin, and therefore they attributed this miracle to Christ. Yet, interestingly, there is no evidence that even one Jewish Rabbi expected the Messiah to be born of a virgin. Of a maiden yes, but of a virgin, no. We might think they should have thought so, but they didn't.

Both of these views accuse Mary of being a sexually active teenager. But these speculations overlook the fact that Luke was a careful historian who explicitly says he investigated every-thing, very probably talking to Mary directly to get the story from her. If she had been lying about her pregnancy, he would have known. Of course, Joseph would also have known the truth. For that matter so would many of the people in Nazareth.

The early Christians had a passion to spread the Christian faith. They certainly would not have encumbered the narratives about Christ with a shoddy story that they would have suspected no one would believe. They believed it and others did too, be-cause it had the earmarks of authenticity. It's not the similarities to legends that impress us; it is the *dis*similarities.

Let's take a closer look at a contemporary version of the theory that the virgin birth was made up by the writers.

The Accounts Have a Hidden Meaning

John Shelby Spong is Bishop of Newark in New Jersey. His new book, *Born of a Woman: A Bishop Rethinks the Birth of Jesus,* is another attempt to, in his words, "rescue the Bible from fundamentalists." He argues that (1) the birth narratives in the New Testament are fanciful stories which are not to be taken literally; and, (2) that Mary was quite likely the victim of rape; and, (3) the virgin birth has contributed immeasurably to an artificial and destructive view of women because Mary has been used to force women to fit into the stereotyped role of mother-hood; and, (4) Jesus was probably married, most likely to Mary Magdalene.[1]

Spong grew up as a biblical fundamentalist, loving the Bible with his very being. When he abandoned fundamentalism, he did not stop loving the Bible, he says, but he simply ceased interpreting it literally. To hear him tell it, this nonliteral method has given him a new appreciation for the Bible's deeper meaning.

So we must ask, did the authors of the gospel accounts simply intend for us to "probe, tease, and dissect the sacred story looking for hidden meanings, filling in blanks, and seeking clues to yet-to-be-revealed truth" as Spong says?[2] He argues that the original readers of the gospels would have understood that these were fanciful stories, but a generation hundreds of years later, separated from Jewish religious roots and having a Western-style mind-set, thinks that the accounts either have to be taken literally or else they are overt lies.

"There was nothing objective about the gospel tradition. These were not biographies. They were books to inspire faith," he writes.[3] Matthew and Luke weren't lying because they knew (or at least thought) that nobody would believe them.

Spong is wrong, very wrong about his assumptions. He says that the New Testament writers were actually writing comments about the Scriptures, loose observations they knew were legends. But any impartial student of the New Testament would agree that the authors intended to write a straightforward account of what happened, not a fanciful story to evoke awe and wonder. They were not commenting on Scripture, they were writing it.

Spong does what every liberal theologian does, namely, to rewrite history to make it come out according to his liking. This kind of revisionism is not merely done by those who are interested in advancing a given political theory (Marxism, for example) but also by those who promote a certain religious bent. To revise history if new historical facts have come to light is one thing; to do it because of certain personal presuppositions is quite another.

Here we have the same old dilemma liberals have always had to confront: After stripping Christ of His credentials as a Savior, they are left with nothing worth believing. Spong began by saying that the virgin birth was never intended to be taken literally, but to inspire faith. Faith in what?

He says the account was written to "inspire and create awe and wonder" but as for me, the "awe and wonder" evaporates very quickly if the accounts are not true. We are left with a Christ whose father was a rapist, a Christ who was probably married, a Christ who is a sinner just like the rest of us. We certainly don't have a Savior.

This is not scholarship, this is unbelief. Spong is absolutely insistent that the Jesus of the gospels be reduced to a mere man. He has chosen to deny the virgin birth (and other miracles) simply to make the accounts conform to his unbelief. He denies the virgin birth because he denies the incarnation, or at least reinterprets it to empty it of its significance. Like all liberals, his conclusions are based on what he believes God cannot do.

Forget the old line that whether or not you believe in the virgin birth is a matter of interpretation. The Bible is not a book that can be interpreted in any way one chooses. Certainly there is honest disagreement over some texts and even issues of doctrine. But the virgin birth and miracles of Christ are clear and unambiguous. The question is whether we are willing to believe them. Unbelief has driven Spong to his views, not an even-handed attempt at interpretation.

Spong has an agenda that comes through clearly on every page of his writings. Though I have never met him, his book tells me nothing worthy of Christ, but much about himself. For example, I know that Spong is in favor of gay rights, because in a previous book, *Rescuing the Bible from the Fundamentalists,* he argues for more tolerance toward the gay community and suggests that the apostle Paul was a homosexual.[4] I also know that he is a feminist, because he says the virgin birth is partly to blame for the suppression of women (presumably because it gives the impression that child-rearing is a high calling). I know much about how he dislikes fundamentalists, and how much he likes giving everything a sexual twist. I know how much (or how little) he believes.

Spong has taken the Jesus of the New Testament and made Him fit into his own personal notion of what Jesus should be. In this book I meet Spong, but I do not meet Christ. Unwittingly, the bishop has simply written his own biography!

In discussing his views he writes, "I will not allow *my* Christ to be defined inside a killing literalism . . ." (italics added).[5] He says he will not subject *his* Christ to literal interpretations. But who is *this* Christ? How do we know that *his* Christ is the right one? Obviously he has created his own private Jesus who is not accessible to everyone. Spong should have entitled his book, *My Very Own Jesus—The Private Beliefs of a Bishop Now Made Public.*

When Spong entices us with a web of speculation about Jesus marrying Mary Magdalene, he reveals his method of biblical interpretation. In a perceptive critique entitled *Who Was Jesus?*, N. T. Wright shows that Spong has cut himself off from all serious historical study in order to open himself up to "a world where the modern exegete can construct a fantasy-history in the interests of a current ideology, in Spong's case a resolute insistence of bringing issues of sexuality into everything."[6] At last he has come full circle: Having assumed that Matthew and Luke invented stories to reflect their own ideologies, so Spong now invents stories to promote his own ideologies.

If Spong thinks that his books will "rescue Jesus from the fundamentalists" (that's probably us, friends), he should know that these tired liberal objections to a miraculous Christ have been answered many times by capable scholars. To think that his book will extinguish the faith of true believers is to believe one can put out a fire with straw!

THE RESULTS OF THE VIRGIN BIRTH

We find it hard to believe that the mother of Alexander the Great became pregnant when she ate a pomegranate, not only because the story has the ring of legend, but because there is nothing else in the life of Alexander to suggest that he was anything other than a man. No historian attributes to him the ability to forgive sins or raise the dead.

But when we think of the larger context of Christ's death and resurrection (yet to be considered), our closed view of the universe breaks open. Unbelief is squeezed from our hearts and we are brought to the realization that this miracle is consistent with the rest of Christ's career. The more we know of Christ the more reasonable the virgin conception becomes.

Here are some results of the virgin birth.

Prophecy Was Fulfilled

Isaiah predicted, "Behold a virgin will be with child and bear a son, and she will call his name Immanuel" (7:14). That word *virgin* (*Almah* in Hebrew) can also be translated "young woman." But interestingly, the Septuagint, a Greek translation of the Old Testament completed in about 200 B.C. and used during the time of Christ, translates it *virgin*. Matthew also uses the Greek work *parthenos,* which can only be translated *virgin.* He is careful to tell us "before they were brought together she was found to be with child by the Holy Spirit."

No detail is overlooked in making us understand that Christ was virgin born. Matthew writes in His genealogy, "and to Jacob was born Joseph the husband of Mary, *by whom* was born Jesus, who is called Christ" (1:16; italics added). In English the pronoun "whom" can refer to either a man or a woman, but the Greek language specifies the gender. Although in Jewish tradition the genealogy is always passed through the father and not the mother, the phrase "by whom" used here is feminine. Matthew wants us to be clear that Christ did not have a human father.

A Sinless Savior Was Born

The virgin birth and Christ's mission as a Savior are linked in the message of the Angel to Joseph. Mary would conceive by the Holy Spirit "and you shall call His name Jesus, for it is He who will save His people from their sins" (Matthew 1:21). His name was *Jesus,* which means, "Jehovah is Salvation." His credentials enabled Him to live up to His name.

His Holiness, the Dalai Lama, does not live up to his name and he knows it. One woman who shook hands with him at the parliament ran back to touch us to "share his energy." I said, trying to smile but still hoping she would get the point, "Why are you doing this? Do you not realize that he is a sinner like the rest of us, and if he doesn't have a sinless Savior he's in big trouble?"

Let's judge the Dalai Lama by his own words. He is believed to be the fourteenth reincarnation from Buddha. In an interview "His Holiness" said, "I'm not the best Dalai Lama there ever was, but I'm not the worst either!"[7] How should we interpret this candid remark? If you're grading on the curve, does it sound like a B + or perhaps even a C? Men may call him "His Holiness," but even he knows better than that. He's just a sinner like the rest of us.

I'm told that in a cemetery there is a tombstone: "Sacred to the memory of Methuselah Koking, died at 6 months." With a name like that we would have expected a long life, but among mortals the best of names does not guarantee the best of lives. Christ was given a name that conveyed awesome credentials but He does not disappoint us.

Scan the religious horizons; go to the library and read all about the great religious teachers of history. Read not simply what they taught but what they had to say about themselves. Look not for a prophet, for their name is legion, but find a Savior, a qualified *sinless* savior. You will discover that Christ has no competitors. If there were another who claimed sinlessness, we would be glad to check out his credentials to see how they compare with Christ's. Mention the requirement of sinlessness and the religious field clears; only one man is left standing. Christ lives up to His name!

"For it was fitting that we should have such a high priest, holy, innocent, undefiled, separated from sinners and exalted above the heavens; who does not need daily, like those high priests, to offer up sacrifices, first for His own sins, and then for the sins of the people, because this He did once for all when He offered up Himself" (Hebrews 7:26, 27).

Notice these observations.

1. Christ is sinless; though He is one with us in His humanity, He has the holiness we lack.

2. He, unlike other priests, did not have to offer a sacrifice for Himself; we need a sacrifice, He did not.

3. His sacrifice was perfect, so he needed to offer Himself but once. If His sacrifice had been tainted with sin, the Father would have rejected it and we would have been left unredeemed.

What is the result of this perfect sacrifice? "Hence, also, He is able to save forever those who draw near to God through Him, since He always lives to make intercession for them" (7:25). Christ is not only able to save great sinners, but He saves us completely, or eternally. And who benefits from His salvation? Given what we know about Him, it makes sense that the benefit is limited to those who "come unto the Father through Him."

Now we understand why Christ is the only way; no one else qualifies. We also understand why other religions can have prophets, but they cannot have a Savior. They do not have a man who has personally triumphed over the influence and consequences of his own sin. The various other religious leaders of the world are drowning men shouting swimming instructions to other weak and drowning men.

Napoleon may not have understood the full implication of his words, but he is quoted as saying that there is an eternity of difference between Christ and other men. And that difference, I might add, is that He has the credentials of "Saviorhood."

SO CLOSE AND YET SO FAR

How close can you come to admiration and love for Christ and still miss the point of His coming? At the Parliament of the World's Religions, I spoke to a woman who told me that she had come to know Christ through the Urantia book, a book whose authorship is shrouded in mystery (though I have a good idea about how it came about). "At last," this woman said, "I have met Jesus."

Here is her story: She loved Jesus, she said, even before she could read. Her mother would read Bible stories to her, and whenever she heard about Jesus, her heart was warmed. She belonged to a liberal, mainline Protestant church, and she adored her pastor. One Sunday at the age of ten, she chose not to go to children's church but decided to stay in the auditorium to hear her pastor speak. "If I sit at the back and am real quiet, if I keep my hands folded and don't move, they'll let me stay up here with the adults."

Before her pastor began to speak an older lady in the congregation spoke to her harshly, "What are you doing here? You're supposed to be in children's church!" She was terribly hurt. Rather than go to children's church (she says she didn't want to color in those books), she left the church and never returned.

At the age of sixteen, she resumed her quest for truth and became involved with a cult. Their authoritarian attitude and demand for money caused her to leave. Then she was invited to a group that reads the Urantia book and she said, "They gave my Jesus back to me." She asked me if she could read a paragraph from the book to me. She chose a story about the compassion of Christ when He was only twelve years old. Obviously she was touched by His sensitivity.

"I can tell you love Him," I said, noticing the tears that welled up in her eyes.

"Yes, I do love Him," she replied.

"But *why* do you love Him?" I asked.

"I love Him for His compassion, I love Him as my Lord, I love Him as my teacher, I love Him as my friend!" she said, holding her arms tightly across her chest.

I asked, "Do you also love Him as your sinless Savior, as the one who died on the cross and shed His blood to forgive your sins and reconcile you to God?"

She broke eye contact with me, glanced away for a second, and said, "I have never thought of it in those terms."

To which I replied, "If you do not love Him as the One who died on the cross for your sins, you do not love Him for the very purpose for which He came to this earth!" I urged her to love Him as her Savior; to love Him for a reason that corresponds to His name.

Is it possible to love Jesus, even to the point of tears—to love Him with fervor and still be lost forever? Yes. Many love Christ for reasons that miss the central purpose for His coming. Ultimately, it is not even love for Christ that saves us, it is faith in Christ; faith for the *right* reason in the *right* Christ that gives us a *right* standing with God the Father.

What a pity to know Shakespeare, but not as a man of literature; to know Newton, but not as a scientist; but what an eternal tragedy to know Christ, as a friend, as a prophet, as a miracle worker, but not as a Savior!

Spong, who believes Christ was conceived when Mary was raped, has a Christ who stands in need of the very grace He claims to have brought to us. *A sinful Savior is an oxymoron.*

But the Christ of the New Testament does not simply throw us a life vest; He personally lifts us from the morally polluted waters found within our hearts and environment.

I was sinking deep in sin
Far from the peaceful shore
Very deeply stained within
Sinking to rise no more
But the Master of the Sea
Heard my despairing cry
From the waters lifted me
Now safe am I.

Souls in danger, look above
Jesus completely saves
He will lift you by His love
Out of the angry waves
He's the master of the sea
Billows His will obey
He your Savior wants to be
Be saved today!

To love Him is not enough. To admire Him is not enough; we must trust Him with our souls, with our *eternal* souls.

Many prophets, but one Savior.

NOTES

1. John Shelby Spong, *Born of a Woman: A Bishop Rethinks the Birth of Jesus* (San Francisco: Harper, 1992).
2. Ibid., 18.
3. Ibid., 71.
4. *Rescuing the Bible from the Fundamentalists* (San Francisco: Harper, 1991), 116–21.
5. *Born of a Woman,* 12
6. N. T. Wright, *Who Was Jesus?* (Grand Rapids: Eerdmans, 1992), 91.
7. "Faces of the Dalai Lama" in *Quest,* Autumn, 1993, 80.

AN EXTRAORDINARY LIFE—

Who Is the Real Jesus?

If you had chosen to attend the theater in Leipzig, Germany, in 1779, you might have seen the play, "Nathan the Wise," written by the dramatist Gotthold Lessing. This drama was crafted to make the point that the essence of all religions should be human respect and understanding. Christianity, Lessing was at pains to show, has often been cruel and opinionated.

Nathan, a Jew, is the hero of the story which centers in Jerusalem where there is conflict between Christians, Muslims, and Jews. Through clever twists and turns in the plot, we learn that Nathan's adopted daughter, schooled in Judaism, is discovered to be a sister to a knight who is portrayed as a German Christian. But another surprise comes at the end when the father of these two young people was not a German after all, but actually the brother of Saladin, the Muslim military leader of Jerusalem!

The lesson, of course, is that three people each belonging to one of the three major religions were at odds with one another without realizing that they were brother, sister, and uncle. If only we could appreciate the commonality of the larger religious family, factions and religious disputes would end.

Lessing ridicules Christianity because he says it rejects the unity of all men as human beings and tries to impose a partisan, incomplete perception of reality on others. One of the characters says of Christianity, "But tell me when and where this madness. This pious rage to have the better God, and to impose this better God as the best on the whole world, more in its blackest form . . ."[1] Devotion and piety, Lessing says, do not depend on our specific doctrines about God. All that matters is human values and the larger human family.

Though I am sharply critical of Lessing's belief in the essential unity of all religions, I do agree that Christianity, particularly in its misguided medieval form, was often cruel. The Crusades to liberate Palestine from the Turks, the persecution of religious minorities, and the Spanish Inquisition are but a few examples of how barbaric a religion can become when it denies the basic principle of freedom of conscience and the love it claims to promote. Jonathan Swift of *Gulliver's Travels* was right when he said, "We have just enough religion to make us hate, but not enough to make us love one another."

This concession aside, Lessing clearly misunderstood the essence of Christianity when he thought it was just another expression of human values. He was saying, in effect, "I can accept Christianity's ethics, but I cannot accept (or, at least, I don't have to accept) its creeds." One of his critics wrote that Lessing spent all of his life hoping that Christianity was true, yet arguing that it wasn't. Right conduct, not right belief, is all that mattered.

We've already learned that Christianity is a historical religion in the sense that it is based not just on teachings but events; the message of the New Testament is that God has visited our planet to reconcile us to Himself. I've already emphasized that we must be willing to give evidence for our faith by using ordinary, historical methods of investigation. Luke, the historian, said that Christ provided for His disciples many "convincing proofs." This makes Him accessible even to skeptics who are willing to examine the Christian faith.

Lessing, however, stressed that historical investigation is never absolute and therefore concluded that there was really no solid basis for Christian doctrines. What is more, he thought that proper historical investigation would probably show that the New Testament accounts about Christ were embellished. The actual Jesus who lived and died was likely only a man; maybe an exceptional man, but just a man nevertheless. In order to find this man, the real man, Lessing began the "quest for the historical Jesus."

Maybe you've never heard of this search for the Jesus of history or maybe you think it's a topic only for scholars. But at times all of us have wondered whether the disciples just might have made up the miracle stories in the New Testament. Or maybe you've heard someone say, "Some scholars think that we know nothing about the historical Jesus!" Get three people together and you might have five opinions about Christ.

The purpose of this chapter is to:

1. Show why it is impossible to strip the New Testament of its miracles on the premise that Christ was just an ordinary man.

2. Discuss how to tell the difference between the miracles performed by Satan and those performed by Christ.

3. Take a brief look at some of the miracles of Christ to better understand how they help verify His credentials.

THE QUEST FOR THE HISTORICAL JESUS

Miracles seem to be on every page of the New Testament. Whether it is turning water into wine, feeding a multitude with one boy's lunch, healing the sick, or raising the dead—all of these miraculous signs are spelled out in vivid detail. As we look around today, we do not see the same phenomena; though there are some people who claim to have seen miracles, when we check them out we usually have good reasons to be skeptical.

So the question is: *Why should we think that these events happened as the New Testament describes them? Is it even credible that such miracles could occur? Or is it possible that Christ did do some small acts of kindness, some memorable object lessons, and later His enthusiastic followers embellished the stories?*

David Hume, you will recall, argued that miracles were impossible because they were contrary to nature. He insisted that historical study shows there is a uniform testimony against miracles, so he said we shouldn't believe they happened no matter how much evidence there is for them!

But such reasoning is circular: We cannot say miracles didn't happen in the past simply because we don't see them today. If God exists and is worthy of the name, He cannot be held hostage to the very patterns of uniformity He created. The biblical God, at least, is always actively involved in holding the creation together moment by moment. When He does something irregular, we call it a miracle.

So all we can do is to check the available eyewitness accounts to see whether such special interventions have occurred. Rather than discussing whether miracles *can* happen, we simply need to evaluate the evidence to see *whether* they have happened.

But belief in miracles is not easy for us to accept. Some scholars have insisted that we must peel away these sensational wonders and try to get behind the stories to the actual kernel of events that took place in first-century Israel. This, they say, is simply separating the Christ of faith from the Jesus of history. The Jesus of history, the argument goes, was a mere man, whereas the Christ of faith is the person the followers of Christ created and wrote about.

Believe it or not, when the liberals went to work to scrub the miracles out of the New Testament, some thought they were doing Christianity a favor. They pointed out that the miracles were a stumbling block to educated people; if they could construct a nonmiraculous Christ, more would believe! They actually insisted that in losing a miracle-working Jesus, nothing of great importance had been lost. Take the New Testament portrait of Christ, they said, airbrush it clean of any miracles, and sophisticated people could return to the gospels and find benefit in them.

Most of us would want to argue that if Christianity is stripped of its supernatural origins, it would be exposed as a hoax. But the theologians/historians did not reason that way; they wanted to insist that Christ was still special even though He was reduced to being a mere man and the New Testament was filled with myths.

Now, I grant that it is easier to believe the New Testament when it is stripped of miracles. But then the question arises: What is left to believe? Some said that the Sermon on the Mount, His parables and methods of teaching would still remain intact. Then there was the motivation we receive through His selfless example. What is more, the miracle stories (the myths, if you please) could also be reinterpreted and with a bit of ingenuity, rich hidden meanings could be found in them. Jesus miraculously feeding the multitudes may be a metaphor for the risen Christ feeding the faith of His followers. And as for the resurrection itself, it may be symbolic of our own liberation.

Sounds simple, right? Would you believe that this enterprise has ended in confusion and contradictions? Let me explain.

Broadly speaking, there were two kinds of liberals. There were those who wanted to deny the miracles and still speak of Christianity as unique, special in some way. Others who were more honest admitted that once you disbelieved in a miraculous Christ, there was no uniqueness left; in fact, there was really nothing left! Perhaps just a few ethical principles that can be found in all religions. Nothing more.

For example, Thomas Sheehan, a professor at Loyola University, admitted in an interview that most liberal theologians are inconsistent: They disbelieve in a miraculous Christ and yet want to hold Him up to be special; they want to "demythologize" the New Testament (strip it of its myths) and still have Christ on some kind of a pedestal. But this, he shows, is inconsistent and quite impossible.

Sheehan has the courage to take his liberalism where it leads, namely to what amounts to the complete emasculation of Christianity. He calls the gospel accounts propaganda. Stripped of miracles, stripped of Christ's claims, and in the end, stripped of most of His teachings, there is nothing left except love your neighbor and do justice, ideas we could have thought up on our own.[2]

The January 10, 1994, issue of *Time* has an article about the Jesus Seminar, where nearly 100 self-proclaimed authorities on the Bible spent six years of study to identify those sayings in the gospels that they believe Jesus really said. Four different colored balls were used to tally the vote. Each participant dropped a *red* bead into a ballot box for sayings he or she believed were probably authentic. *Pink* beads meant that possibly the saying was authentic; *gray* was for those sayings thought to have been altered by the disciples or early Christians; *black* beads were the strongest no vote.

The results? Only 18 percent of the more than 700 sayings attributed to Christ were considered unquestionably authentic; more than half received the black bead.[3] All sayings in the gospel of John were rejected except one verse, "A prophet has no honor in his own country" (4:4). The Christ of these scholars is indeed a shadowy figure about whom we know nothing. We can appreciate the words of William Temple, Archbishop of Canterbury who said in his day, "Why anyone should have troubled to crucify the Christ of Liberal Protestantism has always been a mystery."

What criterion was used to evaluate Christ's words? They assumed that He spoke only in aphorisms and parables. But how do we know that Jesus spoke only in certain ways and on certain topics? As any student in logic would know, such reasoning is profoundly circular. No historian should begin with his own assumptions about what Christ might or might not have said; honesty requires that he follow the evidence wherever it leads.

Behind these investigations is political correctness, a desire not only to have a human Christ but one who agrees with the liberal agenda. To quote John MacArthur, "they simply dismissed every statement containing a hint of some truth or point of view that is rejected by the political liberals in our culture." The parables of the Good Samaritan, passages critical of the rich, the command to love our neighbors—these received red beads. But passages that call for repentance, affirm Christ's deity, or speak of the need of redemption—those passages were "literally blackballed."[4]

Howard Clark Kee, a New Testament professor emeritus at Boston University, calls the work of the seminar "an academic disgrace" and says that its members "seemed determined to find a Jesus free of such features embarrassing to modern intellectuals, as demons, miracles and predictions about the future."[5]

Why has this attempt, like all the other attempts to find the historical Christ, ended in such failure? It is because Christ's *words* are so closely tied to His *works* that one cannot disbelieve the miracles without undercutting everything else He said and did. The human side of Jesus and the divine side cannot be separated. In the end, everything about Christ is miraculous!

Understandably, every liberal has a different opinion about how best to reconstruct a purely human Jesus. But the task is formidable because there are only subjective criteria to separate the heavenly from the earthly; there is no objective basis to disconnect the human from the divine. As Christ Himself said, "If I told you earthly things and you do not believe, how shall you believe if I tell you heavenly things?" (John 3:12). The Christ of earth and the Christ of heaven are inseparably united.

Noted Tubingen professor, Gerhard Kittel, points out the foolishness of those who think they can separate the Christ of faith from the Jesus of history, "The Christ of faith has no existence, is mere noise and smoke, apart from the reality of the Jesus of history. These two are utterly inseparable in the New Testament. They cannot even be thought apart. . . . Anyone who attempts first to separate the two and then to describe only one of them has nothing in common with the New Testament."[6]

Think about it: Though you may choose to disbelieve the miracles, you are still confronted with Christ's claims to deity, His claims to forgive sin, and whole chapters in which He speaks of His relationship to His Father. What do we do with His teachings about heaven, hell, and judgment? If He was only a man, all of these have to be discarded too. His miracles, teachings, and life are one seamless garment, and no thread can be found to unravel them. As J. Gresham Machen says of Christ's miracles, "They are intimately connected with Jesus' lofty claims; they stand or fall with the purity of His character; they reveal the very nature of His mission in the world."[7]

I've already pointed out in the last chapter that liberals who write about Christ usually tell us much more about themselves than they do about Christ. Speaking of the many attempts to find the historical Jesus in the nineteenth century, the famous humanitarian, Albert Schweitzer, wrote, "Each successive epoch of theology found its own thoughts in Jesus. . . . But it was not only each epoch that found its reflection in Jesus; each individual created Him in accordance with his own character. There is no historical task which so reveals a man's true self as the writing of a life of Jesus."[8]

Just think of what he said, "There is no historical task which so reveals a man's true self as writing a life of Jesus." And yet what shall we make of Schweitzer himself, who wrote a biography of Christ and concluded that He was essentially a deluded figure who behaved in frightening and confusing ways? Insanity, Schweitzer said, accounts for His fantastic claims. Is not Schweitzer condemned by his own words?

In the end, liberals came to their final conclusion: Christ could be remade into whoever they wanted Him to be. They edited Him, censored Him, and disbelieved Him on every count. And since their conclusions were largely based on their own personal presuppositions, there are as many historical versions of Jesus as there are authors who want to write His biography! Just as with Bishop Spong whom we met in the last chapter, these scholars have not written a biography of Christ, they have written a biography of themselves.

Interestingly, no scholar has ever been able to present even a shred of historical evidence for their radical views. Not one scrap of manuscript, not one archaeological find, not one new ancient reference! Of course they did extensive investigation into the life and times of Jesus, looking for clues as to who He really was. But at the end of the day, their conclusions were determined by a bias against miracles, an absolute commitment to making Christ a mere man. Yet, as I have pointed out, after centuries of study, no one has been able to uncover a non-supernatural Jesus.

Why, I might ask, should we believe liberals when we have eyewitness accounts? If there were some reason to think that Matthew, Mark, Luke, and John were sloppy historians who made known historical errors and deceived people by creating fantastic stories, then such liberals might have a point. But in the absence of such evidence, we are on safer ground to believe the men who were there rather than revisionists living twenty centuries from these events.

Stay with me, because at the end of this chapter I will give further evidence as to why we must take the gospel accounts as they are or blindly reject all of them. Neutrality on this point is impossible.

TWO SOURCES OF MIRACLES

Miracles are making a comeback. Here are some sample reports that have recently crossed my desk:

— Benjamin Creme's master told him that Maitreya, or the Christ, would soon begin a series of manifestations of light in different parts of the world; signs of the cross would appear miraculously. Already there have been twelve such sightings in the Los Angeles area.

— Angels are being sighted. Eileen Freeman, who has a master's degree in theology from Notre Dame, keeps track of such sightings and has a close relationship with a guardian angel she calls Ennis. An "Angels and Nature Spirits Conference" was held recently in New Mexico.

— Small groups continue to study "A Course in Miracles," and individuals are reporting results—healing, unexpected wealth, and personal fulfillment.

Miracles are everywhere, and we can expect them to increase. A doctor from the Philippines came to Kamloops, British Columbia, to explain his method of doing surgery to the medical community. He showed films of opening a patient, lifting out the diseased organs, stitching the incision, and then wiping it with a sponge. Incredibly, the skin was completely healed without a trace of the surgery.

Present in the audience was a Bible teacher, Rev. Bill McCloud. He asked, "Jesus Christ the Son of God said, 'Except a man be born again he cannot enter into the kingdom of God'— what do these words mean to you?" The surgeon paused; then speaking in an entirely different voice said, "This is the third time I have visited this planet and I'm not going to answer your question!"[9] End of discussion. End of party.

Christians believe that Satan can perform healing, create lighted crosses in windows, appear as an angel, and make statues cry, but sometimes his miracles are more subtle. A man who was for all practical purposes deaf attended a faith healing service, was slain in the spirit and apparently healed. He tested his hearing at home and was even able to hear a whisper. But when he awoke in the morning, his deafness had returned. One would think that if God had actually done the miracle, it would have lasted for at least twenty-four hours! Certainly God sometimes performs miracles today in answer to prayer, but we must not *assume* that all supernatural acts originate with Him.

Christ taught that in the day of judgment some would be banished from His presence forever though they claimed to do miracles in His name. "Many will say to Me on that day, 'Lord, Lord, did we not prophecy in Your name, and in Your name cast out demons, and in Your name perform many miracles?' And I will declare to them, 'I never knew you; *Depart from Me, you who practice lawlessness*'" (Matthew 7:22–23).

The Pharisees often disputed whether Christ's miracles were from God or the devil. We should give them credit for realizing that miracles can have two radically different sources. Given this ambiguity, what reason did they have to believe that Christ's miracles were performed by the power of God?

First, His miracles were different in kind; there are some things Satan can do, but there are some things he cannot do. For example, Christ said that Satan could not cast out demons (or at least he would not), since this would be working against his own purposes. "And if Satan casts out Satan, he is divided against himself; how then shall his kingdom stand?" (Matthew 12:26).

How can we reconcile this assertion with Christ's words (quoted above) that someday even apostates will claim to have cast out demons? Since we know that they could not have cast out demons by Satanic power, it follows that either they only thought they had cast out demons (and Satan withdrew to give the illusion that he was leaving his victims) or else they only claimed to cast out demons without any evidence to back it up. Only Christ could drive evil spirits from the bodies they inhabited; and I believe only Christ the Creator can grant life to a corpse as He did to Lazarus.

Second, Christ's miracles were always completed. When He healed a blind man, both eyes were able to see; when He healed a paralytic, both feet were given strength. Those who use demonic power often find that their "gift" gives only haphazard results. Sometimes there is a miracle, sometimes not. Often there is partial healing or it may only last for a short time. Christ's miracles were almost always open to verification, even by His enemies.

Third, and most important, Christ almost always clearly interpreted His miracles, consistently pointing to Himself as the Son of God. On those occasions when the miracles were not interpreted, it was because the message was obvious. Miracles were performed not just to attract attention but to teach spiritual truth. Nicodemus, himself a ruler of the Jews, saw this connection between Christ's works and words and commented, "Rabbi, we know that You have come from God as a teacher; for no one can do these signs that You do unless God is with him" (John 3:2). He read the signs and saw that they pointed to a credible conclusion. Later Nicodemus apparently saw Christ as more than simply a teacher but as the very Son of God and believed.

What role do miracles play in confirming that a message or messenger is from God? In the New Testament, John calls miracles *signs;* that is, pointers to the credibility of Christ's life and witness. A sign differs from a poof; a sign needs a context in which it is understood. Signs involve not only the event but also its interpretation.

Tourists know the value of signs. I remember a man confessing that as a boy he had changed the direction of a sign along a highway just for the fun of watching the cars head the wrong direction. Today he is still haunted by the trouble his prank caused motorists. Christ's miracles are signposts pointing to who He was and what He came to do.

We should expect miracles from Christ if He was who He claimed to be. He was bringing about a spiritual revolution that needed careful investigation, and people had a right to expect evidence. He was making claims that needed to be checked out; He needed to prove that there was harmony between His words and His works.

Christ's teachings shattered the religious beliefs of His time. If you were a first-century Jew and sinned, you were to go to the temple to receive forgiveness. Jesus was granting the pardon of God to prostitutes right out on the street. The temple was where Israel's God lived; Christ was offering the Almighty to those who believed in Him no matter where they were. His miracles, particularly the Resurrection, vindicated His claim that from now on He, not the temple, was the place where God truly and uniquely dwelt. He undercut the whole system.[10]

With such a radical message, we would *expect* that Christ would do miracles, not simply to help people but as a sign that He was indeed the Holy One of God. His supernatural claims necessitated some supernatural acts.

A PORTRAIT OF A MIRACULOUS CHRIST

Let's consider a few of the miracles to better understand what they were intended to teach about the One who performed them.

Authority over the Physical Universe

One day Christ asked His disciples to go across the Sea of Galilee while He went up to a mountain to pray. That evening a storm blew across the lake and the disciples were terrified. Christ then walked on the water, spoke to the wind, and said, "Peace be still . . . " Immediately, the storm stopped and a "great calm" came over the sea. The disciples then understood that "this was the Son of God."

At the wedding in Cana of Galilee, the wine ran out. Christ asked that the servants fill the water pots with water and in faith they took the water to the governor of the feast. Instantly the water turned to wine—the best wine he had ever tasted! And when the crowd was hungry, five loaves and two fish were turned into food for five thousand.

What did these miracles teach? At creation God gave Adam authority over the earth and the animals in it. Thanks to the Fall, this dominion was lost. Today natural disasters are a constant reminder that we do not control the world. Nor can we control animals, the food supply, or the weather.

These miracles proved that Christ was able to reclaim what the first Adam had lost. At His command the wind would stop, the fish would come, and the water would be turned into wine. He was not controlled by His environment, but in fact He controlled it.

Christ never misused His awesome power. When He fed a multitude with five loaves and two fish, He asked the disciples to pick up the fragments that had been thrown on the ground. When He and His disciples were hungry as they reached Jacob's well, He sent the disciples into the town to buy food.

Nor did He use His power to "even the score" when He was treated unjustly. He could have called twelve legions of angels to deliver Him from the horror of the cross, but He restrained Himself. He is the only one who contradicts the oft-quoted remark, "Power corrupts and absolute power corrupts absolutely."

This man was not a product of creation but was Himself the Creator. Clearly His origin was not from within the human family but from another sphere. Here was a man who could act like God.

Authority over the Moral Realm

Christ was preaching in the middle of a house when four men brought a paralytic on a stretcher, attempting to get to Him. But the house was so packed that they decided to take the roof off the house and lower their friend so Christ had to pay attention to him.

Christ's first words to the sick man were "My son, your sins are forgiven." Understandably, some of the scribes were upset and asked, "Why does this man speak that way? He is blaspheming; who can forgive sins but God alone?" (Mark 2:7). This was a strong claim to deity, for only God can forgive sins. We can forgive the wrong done to us, but only God can forgive the wrong done to Him.

Christ knew their thoughts and replied, "Why are you reasoning about these things in your hearts? Which is easier, to say to the paralytic, 'Your sins are forgiven'; or to say, 'Arise, and take up your pallet and walk'? But in order that you may know that the Son of Man has authority on earth to forgive sins . . . I say to you, rise, take up your pallet and go home'" (2:8–11).

Don't miss the logic: It is much easier to say, "Your sins are forgiven" than it is to say, "Arise, and take up your pallet and walk." Anyone can say, "Your sins are forgiven," because forgiveness is an invisible miracle that cannot be directly verified. Talk is cheap. But to perform a physical miracle that can be objectively verified is more difficult. Christ's reasoning: Let this *visible* miracle be proof that I have authority over the *invisible* world.

Sin, though not the immediate cause of all illness, is nevertheless the ultimate cause of all human misery. Christ's power over sickness was a strong confirmation that He also had power over sin.

No doubt Christ encountered many blind men, but one especially was used to represent the miracle of conversion. Though the man benefited, Christ's primary purpose was to use physical sight as an illustration of the need of spiritual sight. "For judgment I came into this world, that those who do not see may see; and that those who see may become blind" (John 9:39). And when the Pharisees affirmed that they were not blind, Christ replied, "If you were blind, you would have no sin; but since you say, 'We see,' your sin remains" (v. 41). The Pharisees, by the way, had difficulty believing this miracle even though the man's parents confirmed it.

Christ had the authority to heal spiritual blindness and thereby change the human heart. He also claimed that He would be the judge, the One before whom all would have to give an account (John 5:22–23). No other religion has a leader who claimed the right to speak sinners clean. No other taught that the final destiny of every person would be determined by their relationship with him.

Authority over the Eternal Realm

Like it or not, eternity has been stamped on our hearts. We have a desire for immortality, an innate feeling that we should be in touch with the infinite. Some of Christ's miracles demonstrated His authority, not just over time but over eternity.

Christ raised Lazarus from the dead as dramatic proof that even death itself could not limit His authority. And again His power to grant physical life confirmed His authority to grant spiritual life, "I am the resurrection and the life; he who believes in Me shall live even if He dies, and everyone who lives and believes in Me shall never die" (John 11:25, 26).

When Christ was on the cross, He looked helpless and forsaken. Yet even in the throes of death, He was able to say to the thief next to Him, "Truly I say to you, today you shall be with Me in Paradise" (Luke 23:43). No teacher or guru claimed such authority.

THE PORTRAIT THAT WON'T DISSOLVE

Many years ago a celebrated painting by Burne-Jones named "Love Among Ruins" was destroyed by an art firm that had been hired to restore it. Though they had been warned that it was a watercolor and therefore needed special attention, they used a liquid that dissolved the paint.

Throughout the ages men have taken the New Testament portrait of Christ and tried to reduce its bright hues to gray tints, to sponge out the miracles, to humanize His claims. So far, however, no one has found the solvent needed to neutralize the original and reduce it to a cold dull canvas. No matter who tries to blend its hues with those of ordinary men, the portrait remains stubborn, immune to those who seek to distinguish between the original and a later edition.

Perhaps we can better understand why religious liberals throw up their hands in exasperation and say, "We don't even know if a man named Jesus existed"; or "We know nothing about the Jesus of history." Far from undermining our faith, such a statement actually is a backhanded tribute to Christ!

Remember, as we learned, the liberals had hoped to separate the miraculous Christ of the gospels from the historical Jesus. They thought they could peel away the miracles like an onion and find the mere man; but when they were finished, the historical Jesus seemed to vanish amid a welter of contradictions and arbitrary assumptions. They were faced with a choice: *Either they had to accept Him as portrayed in the New Testament, or they had to confess ignorance about Him.*

Try as they might, they simply could not find a purely human Jesus anywhere on the pages of the New Testament. They could not write His biography by accepting bits and pieces of the gospel accounts. In effect, *they were faced with the stark realization that the gospel portrait is either all true or all false.* Determined that they will not accept a miraculous Christ, they opted for saying there might not have been a historical Jesus at all!

C. S. Lewis in *Screwtape Letters* describes how an older devil counsels his nephew on the value of man's search for the historical Jesus:

> In the last generation we promoted the construction of . . . a historical Jesus on liberal and humanitarian lines; we are now putting forward a new "historical Jesus" on Marxian, catastrophic, revolutionary lines. The advantages of these constructions which we intend to change every thirty years or so are manifold. In the first place they all tend to direct men's devotion to something which does not exist, for each "historical Jesus" is unhistorical. The documents say what they say and cannot be added to; each new "historical Jesus" therefore has to be got out of them by that sort of guessing (brilliant is the adjective humans apply to it) on which no one would risk ten shillings in ordinary life, but which is enough to produce a crop of new Napoleons, new Shakespeares, and new Swifts, in every publisher's autumn list.[11]

I have seen Rembrandt's famous painting "Nightwatch" at the Ryjksmuseum in Amsterdam. If I had suggested to the tour guide that the painting should be redone to conform to my own expectations and tastes, she would have had every right to reply, "This painting is not on trial, you are!"

Just as amateurs are quick to pronounce their verdict when beholding a masterpiece, so men today make superficial judgments regarding Christ. If they would only pause a bit longer, they would soon realize that they, not Christ, are being judged.

When compared with other ancient literature, evidence for the reliability of the Bible is impressive indeed. Archaeology, historical research, and comparative studies have all contributed to our belief that we have in our hands a reliable book that is open to investigation. We do not teach that our faith is based on our subjective experience but on objective data.

Stephen Neil says that he spent an evening with a man who was in Hitler's inner circle. This man claimed that if he had been led blindfolded through ten rooms, he would have been able to recognize the one in which the Fuhrer was standing. There was a power, an energy that radiated from this evil man. There were, he said, only three choices: Leave politics; bump him off; or sell yourself to him, body and soul.

Read the gospels and you will find that Christ radiated power too. In His presence, men either turned away in anger, sought to kill Him, or fell before Him in worship. We've spoken of His works, now let us turn to His words.

NOTES

1. Gotthold Lessing, *Lacoön: Nathan the Wise*, William Steel, ed. (London: Everyman's Library, 1970), 137.

2. Thomas Sheehan, *The Reader*, 21 April 1989, 1–28.

3. *Time*, 10 January 1994, 39.

4. John MacArthur, *Masterpiece* July/August 1991, 2.

5. *U.S. News and World Report*, 1 July 1991, 58.

6. Quoted in *He Walked Among Us*, Josh McDowell & Bill Wilson (San Bernardino: Here's Life, 1988), 136.

7. J. Gresham Machen, *Christianity and Liberalism* (Grand Rapids: Wm. B. Eerdman's Pub. Co., 1923), 107.

8. *The Atlantic Monthly*, 1 December 1986, 43.

9. Information given personally to me by Bill McCloud on September 30, 1993.

10. "The New Unimproved Jesus," *Christianity Today*, 13 September 1993, by N. T. Wright, 26.

11. C. S. Lewis, *The Screwtape Letters*, (London: Geofferey Bles, The Centenary Press, 1961), 117.

AN
EXTRAORDINARY
AUTHORITY—

If God Has Spoken, What Has He Said?

The Swedish film director, Ingmar Bergman, dreamed that he was standing in a great cathedral in Europe looking at a painting of Christ. Desperate to hear a word from outside his own world, he visualized himself shouting, "Speak to me!" Dead silence.

That, we are told, was the motivation for his movie "Silence," which portrayed people who despaired of finding God. In our world, he believed, we only hear ourselves. No voice comes to us from outside the human predicament that can tell us about ultimate reality. When seeking a word from God, we are confronted with dead calm.

Can God speak, or is the universe silent regarding ultimate questions? If God is silent either because He cannot speak or because He will not speak, then regretfully we must accept these conclusions:

First, *we ourselves have to be silent about religion and morality.* We have no fixed reference point by which we can judge the relative value of cruel paganism or morally indifferent secularism. Though it seems plausible that we should be able to agree on some moral measuring stick, at the end of the day it comes down to a matter of personal preference. We are not only ignorant regarding the bigger picture, we are not even sure such a picture exists. And since we don't know where we are going, any road will get us there.

Second, *we must be silent in our quest for justice.* Yes, we can try to rectify whatever we can in our world, but if there is no personal God, we have no assurance that the scales will ever be balanced.

Recently I spoke to a Jewish friend who has abandoned his belief in a personal God. I asked him how it felt to know that Hitler would never be judged for the evil of the Holocaust. He struggled with this conclusion; it gave him some pause to have to admit that death ended it all and there was no final judge to whom mankind must give an account.

Struggle he might. This craving for justice, the desire that the truth will finally triumph, is so deeply entrenched in our hearts that we feel anger—and rightly so—when we think that crimes against humanity will go unpunished. Those who escape the imperfect justice of human courts need fear no divine accounting if a personal God does not exist.

Christianity asserts that there will be an accurate, detailed, and final reckoning of the behavior of every human being who has ever lived. Both grace and divine justice will be put on display as every earthly court case is individually retried and every hidden word and deed brought to light. Either our sin will be accounted for through the just sacrifice of Christ, or we will bear our sin in personal suffering forever. Either way, justice will be so accurately weighed on the balances that throughout eternity the inhabitants of heaven will sing, "Righteous and true are Thy ways, Thou King of the nations" (Revelation 15:3).

In Eastern religions the responsibility for justice is assigned to karma, a cruel impersonal law of retribution. In India this system has kept millions of untouchables in humiliation and poverty based on the theory that they are simply getting what they deserve because of sins committed in a previous existence. There is no grace, no opportunity for personal attention. And no assurance that a divine judge has made His decision fully aware of all the facts.

Third, if God is silent, *we must quench our longing for ultimate reality.* Without a personal God we are consigned to a fruitless attempt to make the best of our few short years. We are confined to our personal, distorted, and often conflicting inner experiences. Like an ant walking across a Rembrandt painting, we see the change of color beneath our feet, we feel the roughness of the canvas, but we have no idea what the picture is all about.

Christianity asserts that God is not only capable of intelligent speech but has actually chosen to speak to us. This claim must be distinguished from the gurus who tell us that they speak in behalf of the gods; such prophets are simply trying to interpret what they have experienced of the divine. Men report on their search for the Ultimate, but in Eastern religions the Ultimate itself does not speak. The Hindu can speak of many *avatars* (revelations) because none of them is part of public history; they are all ideas of the mind.[1] The deities themselves are silent.

J. N. D. Anderson, speaking of the Eastern religions, writes "But a God who speaks in an infinite variety of ways, but never decisively, really throws man back upon himself, for then it is up to man to determine how and where he can reach ultimate truth."[2] Yet even in those religions where the deities do not speak, the gurus try to speak the unspeakable and to know the unknowable.

Like Christianity, Islam is monotheistic, but Islam teaches that God has spoken through prophets, especially Mohammed, though we must remember that his message is contradictory to that of Christ. Another important difference is that Christianity asserts not only that God has spoken through messengers, but that *He Himself became the messenger.* The message and the messenger were the same person.

GOD HAS SPOKEN THROUGH CHRIST

Yes, God has spoken through the light of nature which displays His power and glory, but such revelation is open to a wide variety of interpretations. "The heavens declare the glory of God," but they don't necessarily tell us that He is love, nor do they explain how we can be reconciled to Him. To communicate detailed information and to minimize the possibility of misunderstanding, God chose to speak through actual human languages. And what is more, at a point in time He came to personally deliver the message!

We read, "God, after He spoke long ago to the fathers in the prophets in many portions and in many ways, in these last days has spoken to us in His Son, whom He appointed heir of all things, through whom also He made the world. And He is the radiance of His glory and the exact representation of His nature, and upholds all things by the word of His power. When He had made purifications of sins, He sat down at the right hand of the Majesty on high" (Hebrews 1:1–3).

When Christ appeared, there was an explosion of revelation. He is God's final and most complete message to mankind. When John described Him, he borrowed the Greek term *logos* (from which we get *logic),* to communicate Christ's rationality and intelligibility. "In the beginning was the Word *[logos],* and the Word was with God, and the Word was God" (John 1:1). This is a word that can be grasped, a word fraught with clarity and meaning.

At a Bible study I met a Jewish woman, Adrienne Wassink, who told how desperately she had prayed every day that she would find the truth about how to have a personal relationship with God. The very thought that Christ might indeed be the Son of God, the Messiah, frightened her. "O God," she often prayed, "please be anyone but Jesus!"

But at the end of her search, she says, her worst fear came to pass: *God turned out to be Jesus!* There are some good reasons to believe that she is right. Since Christianity makes the astounding claim that "God was in Christ reconciling the world unto Himself," we must take a few moments to consider what Christ actually said. Most important, we must see what He said about Himself.

Christ Claimed to Be God

"Truly, truly, I say to you, if anyone keeps My word he shall never see death" (John 8:51). The Pharisees who heard these words could not believe their ears. A man who was perhaps thirty years old was promising that those who believed in Him would have eternal life. These seemed like the words of a lunatic, so they responded accordingly:

"You have a demon. Abraham died, and the prophets also; and You say, 'If anyone keeps My word, he shall never taste of death.' Surely You are not greater than our father Abraham, who died? The prophets died too; whom do You make Yourself out to be?" (vv. 52–53).

Christ simply replied that His critics really did not know God as they claimed; for if they did, they would know who was speaking to them. He went on to say, "Your father Abraham rejoiced to see My day; and he saw it, and was glad" (v. 56).

"You are not yet fifty years old, and have You seen Abraham?" they replied angrily.

Then came the clincher, "Truly, truly, I say to you, before Abraham was born, *I AM*" (v. 58).

The Jews knew that Christ had often claimed to be God. Now even the incredulous realized that His words could be interpreted in no other way. He had identified Himself with the "I AM," Jehovah who appeared to Moses in the burning bush (Exodus 3:14).

Now if He wasn't God; if He was only a man, this was the highest blasphemy. So the Jews did what they should have done with a blasphemer; they gathered stones to stone Him. Little wonder Christ caused such a stir!

Sometime later when Christ was standing before the high priest, He was asked pointedly, "Are You the Christ, the Son of the Blessed One?" To which He replied, "I am; and you shall see the Son of Man sitting at the right hand of the Power, and coming with the clouds of heaven." Blasphemy again! Unless, of course, He actually was God (Mark 14:61–62).

And what shall we make of His statement, "For not even the Father judges anyone, but He has given all judgment to the Son, in order that all may honor the Son, even as they honor the Father. He who does not honor the Son does not honor the Father who sent Him" (John 5:22–23). Day after day, Christ spoke words which only God could speak and did works that only God could do. A prophet might do some miracles, but only God can forgive sin. Only God can judge human beings after death. Obviously, Christ did not see His audience as potential equals as the New Agers would have us believe.

A Hindu might accept Christ as yet another incarnation of whatever God or gods there be, but as Ghandi put it, He cannot be given a solitary or supreme throne. But it is precisely such solitary preeminence that Christ claims: If there is but one God and Christ is the second person of what we call the Trinity, there cannot be other thrones which He must share. The deity of Christ is the foundational rock of the Christian faith. Affirm it and Christ stands alone without a single rival on the horizon; deny it and Christ is reduced to a foolish prophet who was deluded about His own person and mission. If He was not the one personal God manifest in the flesh, He was a mere man who falsely claimed to do what only God can do; a deceitful man who misled his followers, promising more than He could ever deliver.

The deity of Christ rends a clean and unbridgeable chasm between Christianity and other religious options. And for reasons that will become clear, it also means that other religions cannot logically claim Christ as one of a long line of prophets. Islam, for example, professes great respect for Christ. Indeed, many Muslims will affirm that Christ is one of the great prophets that preceded the greatest prophet, Mohammed. They admire Christ, but they do not worship Him.

Muslims believe that the one unforgivable sin is associating anyone or anything with the Almighty, and so the very idea of an incarnation is anathema. They think therefore that Christians have taken a man and made him into God. As Anderson says, "They find it desperately difficult to realize that in fact the movement in Christianity, is not up but down: not exalting a man and equating him with God, but worshipping a God who became man."[3]

At the Parliament of the World's Religions, delegates received a copy of an official address from the Moslem Society of the USA. It said that the tribulation of Dajjal is the greatest of all tribulations, "There is no tribulation greater than that of the Dajjal from the creation of Adam to the Day of Resurrection." But in the Koran, there is one that is greater and that is the deity of Christ. To quote the speech:

> . . . the holy Quran speaks of another great tribulation in the form of the Christian doctrine relating to the Divinity of Christ. It denounces this doctrine in the strongest terms as the greatest of all tribulations for humanity. . . . The heavens may almost be rent thereat, and the earth cleave asunder, and the mountains fall down in pieces, that they ascribe a son to the beneficent! Thus the doctrine of the Divinity of Jesus, according to the Quran cannot be ascribed to Christ but to Antichrist.[4]

There you have it. The Koran is quite right in this regard: The divinity of Christ sharply divides Christianity from all of the other religions of the world. This is the great divide, the unbridgeable chasm, a gulf that extends from here to eternity. If it is false, it is worthy of great tribulation and a curse; if it is true, it is the best news—perhaps the only really good news—available on planet earth.

Clearly, this is further evidence that the God of the Bible and Allah are not the same deities with just different names. Islam denies the Trinity and must therefore deny the deity of Christ. Christianity teaches that God could become man and still be ruling the universe during the life of Christ, because though God is one unified being, He is three personalities. Salvation, therefore, can be of the Lord since God the Son paid a ransom to God the Father (as will be explained in the next chapter).

Since Christ claimed to be God, it follows that He would assert exclusivity. He taught that He alone was the way to God; He alone was qualified to be our sin-bearer. He affirmed that the eternal destiny of men and women depended on their relationship to Him.

Christ's Claim to Exclusivity

After Christ told the disciples that He was going away, Thomas asked Him a question. "Lord, we do not know where You are going; how do we know the way?"

Christ's response was to the point: "I am the way, and the truth and the life; no one comes to the Father, but through me" (John 14:6). All attempts to reinterpret this verse to blunt its meaning have been contrived; they fail because the words are so clear, so consistent with the rest of Christ's teachings.

a. *The Way*

If you are traveling between Chicago and Dallas, highway signs are important. You are, of course, free to take any road you wish as long as you either don't care or don't know where you are going. No intelligent person is indifferent to geographical directions; nor should we be indifferent to the spiritual road map Christ outlines. Contrary to most other optimistic teachers, He did not teach that there were many ways to the divine.

We've all had the experience of asking directions in a strange city only to be told that we were talking to another stranger to the city. Or else we meet someone who knows our destination only too well but gives directions too complicated to follow. How we wish that our guide would just go with us to show us the way, step by step.

A visitor standing in the desert asked his Arab guide, "Where is the path?" to which the guide replied, "I am the path." If it is foolish to begin a trek through the mountains in the desert without a reliable guide, why do we think that we can manage spiritual terrain on our own? Christ is invisible to us but real; He is both map and guide, both friend and leader.

When Christ becomes our Savior, He receives us as we are. He takes us by the hand on our very first step toward our destination. No matter our predicament, we do not have to find our way out of it alone. He is at our doorstep ready to take us where we need to go.

And to where does He lead us? In this life we are reconciled to our Father, and in the life to come we are escorted directly to the Father's house. Philip, standing next to Christ, longed for a theophany to bolster his faith, "Lord, show us the Father, and it is enough for us" (John 14:8). Interestingly, Christ did not chide him for wanting more information, but He did chide him for not realizing that all the information he needed was standing before him, "Have I been so long with you, and you have not come to know Me, Philip? He who has seen me has seen the Father; how do you say 'Show us the Father'?" (v. 9).

Imagine! *To see Christ the visible man is to see the invisible God, the Father!* Little wonder Christ can lead us all the way from the city of destruction to the celestial city. Only He is qualified to take us all the way home.

Error does have this advantage over truth: There are many ways to be wrong, but there is only one way to be right. Error is of necessity always broader than truth. When we meet someone who believes that all paths lead to God, we should have the presence of mind to realize that only error could have such flexibility; error can encompass any spectrum that is not occupied by truth. Our world is filled with guides who claim to know something the rest of us don't. Hundreds of false teachers have gathered followings but in the end have been shown to be just as fallible as those who followed them. Death proved them to be as vulnerable as the rest of us to the limitations of humanity.

b. *The Truth*

Gotthold Lessing, whom we met briefly in the last chapter, said that if God were to offer him complete truth with his right hand and the unending search for truth with the left, he would take the left hand even if it meant he would always be in error. His premise was that the journey to find truth is more important than the destination!

Lessing for all his brilliance was a fool. For openers, if he had no truth at all, he couldn't even distinguish degrees of truthfulness. He couldn't even know if his search was leading him in the right direction because he wouldn't know what he was looking for! Second, he didn't realize that error can be costly. Even a little bit of truth is better than an ongoing quest.

Knowing the truth about poison, a faulty parachute, or even the direction of an expressway is preferable to an endless search for truth. If it is best to know the truth about the mundane matters of this life, how much more important it is to know the truth about the bigger questions of life. Christ taught that Lessing's eternal destiny (and that of everyone else) depends on whether he found the truth and believed it.

In claiming to be the truth, Christ goes beyond the prophets who simply said they were speaking the truth. Like the wings of an airplane, Christ's life and lip were in complete harmony. He claimed reliability; He will not mislead us. When He opened His mouth, His words were carefully chosen and guaranteed by the God of the universe. If He were to tell a lie, God Himself would be implicated in evil. He could not afford to be wrong even once.

Consistency is another word to describe Christ. You could study math or chemistry from a person whose character was questionable. But it would be hypocritical to hear a greedy man plead for generosity or an immoral person extol the virtues of purity.

Christ taught that God's standard for us was purity in thought, word, and deed; and though we cannot live up to this perfection, He did. He had authenticity; He was believable. He is the truth objectively; He does not simply become the truth for those who believe on Him. He would be the truth even if everyone rejected Him. Remember, as we learned in chapter 2, truth has universality; so although we are entitled to our own opinions, we are not entitled to our own truth!

c. *The Life*

What did Christ mean by claiming to be "the life"?

He is, of course, the author of physical life. Like the moon depends on the sun, so the universe depends on the Son for its existence and upkeep. He is the creator and sustainer, moment by moment "upholding all things by the word of His power."

He is also the author of spiritual life, a quality of existence that He has within Himself. Let's not confuse this eternal life with eternal existence. All people have eternal existence (some, unfortunately, will exist in separation from God in hell), but only those who believe in Christ have a quality of life called "eternal life." In fact, He has eternal life within Himself and bestows it on those who believe in Him. "For just as the Father has life in Himself, even so He gave the Son also to have life in Himself" (John 5:26). Elsewhere, He claims to have the words of eternal life (John 6:68).

When Christ added "No man comes to the Father but through me . . . ", He narrowed the gate, He built a fence around the road, and He pointed to where the path led. We have no right to try to tear down the gate posts, make the road broader, and choose a destination according to our own liking. All other paths lead somewhere else; they go away from the Father, not toward Him.

Earlier in His ministry He declared, "I am the door; if anyone enters through Me, he shall be saved, and shall go in and out and find pasture. The thief comes only to steal, and kill, and destroy; I came that they might have life and that they might have it abundantly" (John 10:9, 10). He certainly did not teach that it doesn't matter which path you take or which teacher you follow. Since there is truth, there is also error.

Christ taught that there were two paths, an attractive broad way that led to destruction and the narrow way that often was overlooked. "Enter by the narrow gate; for the gate is wide, and the way is broad that leads to destruction, and many are those who enter by it. For the gate is small, and the way is narrow that leads to life, and few are those who find it" (Matthew 7:13, 14). The broad way is deceptive because many so-called enlightened religious leaders have labeled it the way to life. Christ confronted us with two paths, with two separate gates and two separate destinations.

If these claims are true, the implications shatter the fabric of our present religious environment.

THE IMPLICATIONS

If we take Christ's words at face value, where does this lead us? We are forced to reach these conclusions.

1. *Christ is the final and most complete revelation from God.*

Perhaps you have wondered whether Christ could be combined with some religion such as the Muslim faith which teaches that both Christ and Mohammed are prophets of God. Or, what about the Baha'i faith which teaches that Christ was the right prophet for His times, but as the centuries progressed we needed a fresh revelation through Bahá ú lláh?

One reason Christ must stand alone, and be accepted or rejected on His own merits, is that these so-called later prophets teach doctrines that are in direct conflict with His teachings.

Let's use Bahá ú lláh (founder of the Baha'i faith, born in Persia in 1817) as an example of how incompatible other religions are with Christ. Bahá ú lláh claimed that his vision of the nature of man and society superseded the teachings of Christ. Children, the argument goes, need information that is suitable for them; so do teenagers and adults. He claimed to be God's messenger for this age of human maturity, originating a unified religious system. He had, he says, a dialogue with the Holy Spirit of God, giving revelation on a whole range of religious issues.

Bahá ú lláh believed that previous messengers of God are agents of an unbroken process, the awakening of the human race to its spiritual and moral potentialities. His writings stress the themes of justice, unity, and love. Could it be that he received a more recent revelation from God? Did he have more direct contact with the Almighty than Christ?

Clearly, both Christ and Bahá ú lláh could not be speaking in behalf of the same changeless God. Here are some of Bahá ú lláh's teachings.[5] Look at this contrast.

a. It was God's will to effect a change in the character of humankind by developing the moral and spiritual qualities that are already latent within the human soul.

Compare Christ's words, "For from within, out of the heart of men, proceed the evil thoughts, fornications, thefts, murders, adulteries, deeds of coveting and wickedness, as well as deceit, sensuality, envy, slander, pride and foolishness. All these evil things proceed from within and defile the man" (Mark 7:21–23). These are two incompatible teachings of what lies "latent in the human soul."

b. Those who believe in God's unity should not use doctrinal convictions to discriminate between those whom God has used as channels of light.

Listen to Christ's words, "Truly, truly, I say to you, he who does not enter by the door into the fold of the sheep, but climbs up some other way, he is a thief and a robber. . . . All who came before Me are thieves and robbers, but the sheep did not hear them" (John 10:1, 8). Whole chapters in the New Testament are devoted to instructions on how to identify and deal with false teachers. Indeed, doctrinal discrimination is a mark of spiritual maturity.

c. Religion was in a state of evolution, and the time had now come when man could see the entire panorama of the earth's spiritual development. New revelations about the global spiritual unification of humanity is an immediate possibility.

Take a moment to reread Matthew 24 to see Christ's vision of the future. In the end time there will be war, famine, earthquakes, treachery, and the persecution of God's people. Interestingly, He adds, "And many false prophets will arise, and will mislead many" (v. 11). And again, "For false Christs and false prophets will arise and will show great signs and wonders, so as to mislead, if possible, even the elect" (v. 24).

Bahá ú lláh and Christ saw the future very differently.

d. The purpose of all past revelations is to prepare the human species as a single organism capable of taking up the responsibility of its collective future.

Compare the words of Christ, "But when the Son of Man comes in His glory, and all the angels with Him, then He will sit on His glorious throne. And all the nations will be gathered before Him; and He will separate them from one another, as the shepherd separates the sheep from the goats; and He will put the sheep on His right, and the goats on the left" (Matthew 25:31–33).

According to Christ, the revelations from God are to prepare us for eternity and to help us avoid the religious deception that will engulf the earth. We will not take up the responsibility for our collective future, but rather the whole world will be judged by God.

Virtually all false teachers agree with the doctrines of Antichrist, namely, the perfectibility of human nature, a vision of a utopia that will be the result of our own collective efforts. Just let us come together minimizing our differences and accentuating our similarities, and a future of peace and prosperity awaits us.

The New Testament teaches that for a brief time men will succeed in building a worldwide, unified religion. Antichrist will be worshiped for bringing economic stability and peace to the earth. There will be signs and wonders and a giddy optimism about humankind's transformation into a new era. But Christ will return as judge of all men, and those who have rejected Him will suffer justly.

Say whatever you say about Bahá ú lláh, he is not on a continuum with Christ. Logically, both Bahá ú lláh and Christ may be wrong, but both cannot be right. These so-called later revelations cannot be another step in God's progressive revelation but must originate from an entirely different source. The choice is between Christ and a prophet who is walking on a different road.

There is a second reason why the evolutionary view of religion evaporates under scrutiny. No one in the universe can claim to be qualified to give a more complete revelation than Christ. Is there a new prophet who is closer to God than He? *Is there the slightest possibility that a prophet has arisen who is better at revealing God than God Himself?*

To quote Stephen Neill:

[Christian faith] maintains that in Jesus the one thing that needed to happen has happened in such a way that it need never happen again in the same way. . . . The bridge has been built. There is room on it for all the needed traffic in both directions, from God to man and from man to God. Why look for any other?[6]

In discussion with a member of the Baha'i faith, I pointed out that Bahá ú lláh was disqualified because his teachings contradicted those of Christ. "Are you saying God can't speak today?" he asked, thinking that my convictions put arbitrary limits on God. "Of course God can speak whenever He wants to," I said, "but when the sun comes out there is no need for the stars."

Today people speak about moving beyond Christianity to something better. New Agers say that Christianity is like a boat that is necessary to take you across the river, but once you disembark you are free to transcend it and enter into a whole new existence. Christianity is the baby steps, but then we must move on to something more mystical, satisfying, or complete. But as someone has said, to move beyond love is to lust; to move beyond rationality is to go to insanity, and to move beyond medicine is poison. And to move beyond Christianity is to move to error and gross deception. Christ is the one man you can never get beyond without falling into a deep pit.

Strictly speaking it is not possible to move beyond Christianity; *you must abandon Christianity to move beyond it!* Whenever you try to add to Christianity you subtract from it. Just as wine is diluted with every drop of water, so the power of the gospel must remain distinct or be reduced to something it was never meant to be. Those who surrender the uniqueness of Christ do not simply surrender a part of the Christian message, but they surrender it entirely. We cannot remove the foundation and profess that the building is still intact.

"I am the Alpha and the Omega," says the Lord God, "who is and who was and who is to come, the Almighty" (Revelation 1:8). Alpha was the first letter of the Greek alphabet, Omega was the last. All the information in *The Encyclopaedia Britannica* is written with only twenty-six letters of the alphabet. So Christ is the A to Z, and He contains in Himself everything we need to know about God and His relationship to the world. The moment we accept a more recent revelation, we turn away from Him to follow another path.

2. *Christ gives us the criterion by which all other worldviews can be judged.*

We might be like ants on a Rembrandt painting, but if we are in communication with the artist, He can tell us what the painting represents. And though we see through a glass darkly, we do see. We know where we came from; we know where we are going; and we have some understanding of the purpose of it all.

Our task is not to try to make Christ harmonize with our opinions; we have no right to correct His teaching. We should not be more broadminded than He.

On a plane I met a man with whom I had a lively discussion. It went something like this:

"As far as I'm concerned, as long as we are sincere in what we believe, it doesn't matter to God what religion we have."

"Really?" I replied, "If what you are saying is true, we should try to do all we can to get this message out to America. Maybe I can write a book, maybe I can preach a series of messages explaining this teaching to people."

He genuinely seemed interested.

"But I do have a question that has to be answered first," I continued. "How do you know that it doesn't matter what a person believes, just as long as he is sincere?"

"Well, that's *my* opinion," he confidently replied.

"Your opinion!" I said, letting a smile blunt the force of the remark that was to come, "Opinions are a dime a dozen. . . . I thought maybe you were going to tell me that you had a revelation from God, because *only He would know what we have to do to get to heaven!* Maybe you didn't realize you claimed you were speaking on His behalf!"

"Then how can you be so sure *your* opinion is right?" he asked with a kind of finality. "Did *you* receive a revelation from God?"

"Neither my opinion nor yours matters," I said. "We simply do not have enough information to know the answer to ultimate questions. That's why we have to look to Christ who was God and therefore in possession of all necessary knowledge about God. . . . He had the credentials to prove His claims. We have no right to make the way to heaven any broader than He Himself made it. And He said that those who believed in Him would have eternal life and those who rejected Him would be condemned." As we talked, I think I helped him see the necessity of looking to Christ for answers.

Think of the arrogance of those who think they know better than Christ what God is like! Yes, opinions are a dime a dozen. Opinions might be important in politics, but in religion we need someone who has divine authority. We simply cannot depend on our own hunches; much less should we manufacture ideas about God that are according to our own liking. He does not ask us how to run His universe. Our responsibility is to find out if He has spoken and if so to listen to that voice.

During the Russian revolution of 1918, Lenin said that if Communism were implemented there would be bread for every household, yet he never had the nerve to say, "I am the bread of life; he who comes to Me shall not hunger, and he who believes in Me shall never thirst" (John 6:35).

Hitler made astounding claims for the role of Germany on this planet, believing that he was beginning a thousand-year Reich (rule). Despite these outlandish claims he never said, "He who believes in the Son has eternal life; but he who does not obey the Son shall not see life, but the wrath of God abides on Him" (John 3:36).

Buddha taught enlightenment; yet he died seeking more light. He never said, "I am the light of the world; he who follows Me shall not walk in darkness, but shall have the light of life" (John 8:12).

Mohammed claimed that he and his tribes were descendants from Abraham through Ishmael, another son of Abraham. But he did not say, "Before Abraham was born, I AM" (John 8:58).

Freud believed that psychotherapy would heal people's emotional and spiritual pains. But he could not say, "Peace I leave with you; My peace I give to you; not as the world gives, do I give to you. Let not your heart be troubled, nor let it be fearful" (John 14:27).

New Age gurus say that all of us will be reincarnated, yet not a one of them can say, "I am the resurrection, and the life: he that believeth in me, though he were dead, yet shall he live: And whosoever liveth and believeth in me shall never die" (John 11:25 KJV).

I urge you to face the question: Who then, is Christ? A liar? A lunatic? A legend? Or, Lord? He simply does not allow us the luxury of neutrality.

Poor Ingmar Bergman! He wanted to hear from God, but he sought an answer in the wrong place. Rather than listen for His whisper in an empty cathedral, he should have heard His megaphone on the pages of the New Testament. And, as Christ was fond of saying, "He that has ears, let him hear!"

That Jesus claimed to be God is clear; what is equally clear is that He is the God He claimed to be. In the end as Adrienne Wassink discovered, God turned out to be Jesus. And as the next chapter will show, there is even more reason to listen with care.

NOTES

1. Lesslie Newbigin, "Religious Pluralism and the Uniqueness of Jesus Christ," *International Bulletin of Missionary Research,* April 1989, 52.
2. J. N. D. Anderson, *Christianity and Comparative Religion* (Downers Grove: InterVarsity, 1970), 16.
3. Ibid., 49.
4. Moslem Society of U.S.A. (Chicago: Heaven On Earth Publications, n.d.).
5. *Bahaullah* (Australia: Baha'i Publications, 1991).
6. Stephen Neill, *Crisis of Belief* (London: Hodder and Stoughton, 1984), 31.

AN
EXTRAORDINARY
DEATH—

What Happened on that Middle Cross?

Years ago I was sitting next to a popular woman pastor at a banquet. I asked her, "Do you believe Christ is the only way to God?" She replied, "Of course! Why do you ask?"

Knowing that she was deeply involved in the New Age movement, I persisted, "Do you believe that all the religions of the world are equally valid?" Again the reply, "Of course!" When I asked her how this could be reconciled with the view that Christ was the only way to God, she refused to answer. Undaunted, I persisted until she leaned over and whispered in my ear, "When I speak about Christ, I'm not talking about Jesus of Nazareth!"

She believed in the cosmic Christ who indwells everyone, a universal Christ who unifies the various religious traditions. He is not a Savior but only shows the way; He points to where we should go but makes no claim to take us there.

Thousands of people who believe in Christ will be eternally separated from God because they have believed in the wrong one. The Christ of the New Testament, Jesus of Nazareth, warned that some day there would be many Christs. "Then if anyone says to you, 'Behold, here is the Christ,' or 'There He is,' do not believe him. For false Christs and false prophets will arise and will show great signs and wonders, so as to mislead, if possible, even the elect. Behold, I have told you in advance" (Matthew 24:23–24). The day of false Christs is here.

The New Age movement has taken the Christ of the New Testament and sculptured Him (with a verbal hammer and chisel) into a completely new image which is to their liking. This new sculpture is able to sit on the same display shelf with the sculptures of Buddha, Krishna, and other holy men.

The tools used to remake Christ into this image are (1) discovering "hidden writings" that purport to contain the long-lost truths of the cosmic Christ; (2) transferring primary allegiance from scriptural revelations to new revelations received through channelers and psychics; and, (3) developing an esoteric system of interpreting the Bible that enables the reader to seek hidden meanings so Jesus can be made to appear as a New Age evangelist.[1]

The goal, of course, is to separate Jesus (a mere human vessel) from the Christ (usually divine, but cosmic and impersonal). Some say that Jesus became the Christ through reincarnation; others say that He was initiated in Egypt or India. What's important is that Christ did not come into the world to suffer and die but to release the divine spark of light imprisoned within us. As we seek enlightenment, we can escape from the body at death and be united to the divine.

What do we make of these reinterpretations? Ron Rhodes in his excellent book *The Counterfeit Christ of the New Age Movement* has shown conclusively that there is no credible evidence that Jesus went down to Egypt or Tibet to learn the ancient wisdom of the East.[2] Esoteric interpretations of the New Testament take texts out of context and twist them to fit the New Age image of Christ. The interpretations are so subjective that the Bible can be made to say anything these devotees wish it to say. They use an old trick: Bypass the plain literal teaching of the Bible by finding hidden meanings that support the New Age worldview.

Why would the New Agers expend so much speculation on trying to make Jesus into a cosmic Christ? A cosmic, esoteric Christ does not have to die a shameful death on a cross; he does not shed blood, for there are no hands and feet that can be pierced with nails. This Christ has a broad perspective and embraces the religions of the world. To quote Rudolf Steiner, he "belongs to the whole earth and can enter all human souls, regardless of nation or religion . . . this is the true 'Second Coming.'"[3]

In the New Age movement as in Gnostic literature, Eve and the serpent are the redeemers of mankind. Eve is to be commended for choosing the path of enlightenment, and Satan is to be praised for having offered it to her. God is the tyrant who was rightfully spurned by His creatures. This explains the emphasis on the goddess in the New Age movement: Eve is the goddess who points us to the right path.

David Spangler of the New Age movement says that "any old Christ will not do, not if we need to show that we have something better than the mainstream Christian traditions. It must be a cosmic Christ, a universal Christ, a New Age Christ."[4]

The battle lines are drawn. Will the real Savior please stand up?

The New Testament teaches that Christ and Jesus are the same person. At His birth the angels said, "Today in the town of David a Savior has been born to you; he is Christ the Lord" (Luke 2:11 NIV). Simeon, who held the baby Jesus in his arms, saw "the Lord's Christ" (Luke 2:26). Already in the first century, John speaks directly to those who would separate the cosmic Christ from Jesus the man. "Who is the liar? It is the man who denies that Jesus is the Christ. Such a man is the antichrist—he denies the Father and the Son" (1 John 2:22 NIV).

Contrary to the New Agers, Jesus affirmed that His purpose was to come into the world and die. He perceived that His death was a sacrifice for sins (Matthew 26:26–28). He said it clearly, "the Son of Man did not come to be served, but to serve, and to give His life a ransom for many" (Matthew 20:28). He laid down His life for the sheep (John 10:11). John the Baptist summarized Christ's mission in a single sentence, "Behold the Lamb of God who takes away the sin of the world" (John 1:29). Christ knew that without Him we all would perish, not for lack of enlightenment but for lack of forgiveness.

We come now to another ditch that divides Christianity from other options. All other religions believe that some form of human effort is involved in the salvation process (however that word *salvation* may be defined). Regardless of what they believe about the Religious Ultimate or what they understand salvation to be, other religions teach that we have to save ourselves or at least help God (or the gods) do it.

THE GULF OF CHRISTIANITY

The chasm between Christianity and other religions now expands into a gulf that becomes as wide as eternity. Even the thought of finding some common ground must disappear. The break is as logically complete as it can ever be.

Christianity stands in unbending opposition to any form of the idea that salvation involves our efforts. Christ presented a radical view of sin and an equally radical view of God. By the time this chapter ends, I hope you will agree that what He did for us has nothing in common with other theories of salvation.

Christ was crucified between two thieves. If you had had a video camera, He would have looked like an ordinary man, dying a common though painful death. Yet the New Testament teaches that, invisible to the human eye, a sacrifice was being made for sinners. This death was like no other. Salvation, which Christianity defines as reconciliation with God, was accomplished for those who believe.

Read these seven affirmations and ask: What other religion believes this?

God Alone Planned Salvation

When sin entered the universe through Lucifer and then came to the human family through Adam and Eve, God was not caught off guard. Nor did He simply have to adjust Himself to evil, making the best of His contaminated creation. Even before Creation, God's plan for rescuing fallen man was already in place. Paul wrote, " . . . in the hope of eternal life, which God, who cannot lie, promised long ages ago" (Titus 1:2). Elsewhere we read that He chose those who would be His from before the foundation of the world (Ephesians 1:4). This is further proof, if proof is needed, that salvation was God's plan from eternity past.

In the Garden itself, the Lord said to the serpent, "And I will put enmity between you and the woman, And between your seed and her seed; He shall bruise you on the head, And you shall bruise him on the heel" (Genesis 3:15). Through Christ, God accomplished in time what He had planned in eternity.

What does this say about God? He is personal, a Being who can think, plan, choose, and act. He exists independent of the world as the one infinite God. And thankfully, He is also the searching God.

If religion can be defined as man's attempt to find God, Christianity is not a religion in this sense: Christianity is God coming to search for man. Figuratively speaking, God takes the first steps toward us, then He extends His hand to enable us to take our first step toward Him. If we truly seek Him, it is because He seeks us.

God Alone Initiates Salvation

The plan of eternity past is later executed in God's way and according to His timetable. Christ comes and becomes a sacrifice for sinners. Human merit, all those deeds that make us feel better about ourselves, had to be permanently set aside as a basis for reconciliation with God. From God's viewpoint, we are not filled with latent good but with latent evil. Our hearts, Christ taught, are deceitful, and our moral blemishes can neither be covered nor changed by us or through religious rituals.

I don't mean to imply that we always do bad things, nor are we as bad as we can be. During a particularly severe snowstorm here in Chicago, the media took pains to point out that neighbors help each other, and sometimes people help strangers to survive. Some people are better or worse than others, but deeds of kindness and compassion are found in varying degrees among all the religions of the world. What Christianity asserts is that none of these works is capable of changing God's mind about us and our sin.

Even our good deeds are tainted; our motives are always mixed. There is simply nothing we can do that God will accept. Just as you can add a million bananas and never get an orange, so all human goodness added together will never change God's mind regarding so much as a single sinner. He doesn't accept human righteousness; He only accepts His own.

The Sear's Tower is the tallest skyscraper in Chicago. The owners might be quick to speak proudly about its height in relationship to other buildings. But if the discussion turned to which of the buildings was closest to the farthest star, the Sear's tower would still be first, though the difference in its proximity would be negligible. We, like buildings, are only as tall as our standard of measurement.

We like to think of ourselves as better than others, but when we compare ourselves with God there is little difference between us. We may breathe a sigh of relief when we realize that many people are worse than we are; but such judgments are misleading. We are like the boy who said he was six feet tall, and he was, according to the yardstick *he* had made! We forget that God's holiness is so radically different that no human goodness can approach it. "For there is no distinction, for all have sinned and fall short of the glory of God" (Romans 3:23). God's standard is His glory.

We have nothing in common with the holiness of God. Augustine said, "He who understands the holiness of God despairs of trying to appease Him." The moral gap between us and God is infinite. As Douglas Groothuis says, "Jesus' love cannot be reduced to the desire to see ignorant deities discover their identity and so share in His Christhood. . . . Where the New Age sees a sleeping god, Jesus finds a tempest of transgressions."[5]

In an earlier chapter, I pointed out that if you are drowning you need a qualified lifeguard to lend you a hand. Actually, this understates our predicament. We are not just drowning; we are, spiritually speaking, already dead in trespasses and sins. We don't just need a rope, we need someone to scoop us out of the water and give us life. Other religions take good men and try to make them better, but only Christ takes dead men and makes them alive.

I'm not just saying that we can contribute little to our salvation; we can contribute *nothing* at all. If God did not save, we would never be saved; if He did not reconcile us to Himself, we would never be reconciled.

God Alone Completes Salvation

How can God associate with sinners and still maintain His honor? Years ago some atheists published a tract in which they intended to mock God. They wanted to show that if we are known by our friends, God's reputation is in doubt. Abraham, they pointed out, lied about his wife to save his own skin, and yet he was called "a friend of God." Jacob was a liar and a cheat, yet he is called "a prince with God." David was an adulterer and a murderer and yet he is called, "A man after God's own heart." The atheists asked, *What kind of God would associate with these men and call them His friends?*

In their own perverse way these unbelievers had a point. If we are to judge someone by his friends, God's reputation might be tarnished. So whatever God did to reconcile sinners would have to vindicate His honor. His reputation would have to be preserved and the scandal removed from His name.

Paul wrote that God set forth Christ publicly "as a propitiation in His blood through faith . . . for the demonstration, I say, of His righteousness at the present time, that He might be just and the justifier of the one who has faith in Jesus" (Romans 3:25, 26). God remained just and yet became the justifier of those who believe.

God's holiness could neither be tainted nor compromised to achieve His desired result. He couldn't lower His standards because of love; He couldn't choose to be reconciled to those who were still considered sinners. Nor could He pretend that sin does not exist. Who would meet His requirements? Who could satisfy His justice? Who could appease His outrage against sin?

Only God could meet His own requirements.

God the Father demands perfection which we do not have, but God the Son came to die on the cross to provide this righteousness. He lived a life of perfect obedience and gave a perfect sacrifice which the Father accepted on our behalf. No human works are involved; no human merit can be added to the completeness of Christ's work.

One man may die for another on the battlefield. Or one man may even die for many in the case of a political prisoner being executed as a ransom for his countrymen, but it is unthinkable that one man could die for generations that have not yet been born. Thus when the Bible says that Christ is the "propitiation for our sins; and not for ours only, but also for those of the whole world" (1 John 2:2), it refers to a sacrifice made that reconciles us to God. He died that we might not suffer the ultimate fate that our sins deserve.

Though Christ had personally not committed a single sin, on a cross outside Jerusalem he became guilty of all the perversity we see on our planet. He became legally guilty of rape, child molestation, and lying—He was guilty of all sin before God. No wonder the light of the sun was obscured and darkness fell over the whole earth! The most terrible criminal was dying on the cross. The songwriter reminded us:

> Well might the sun in darkness hide
> And shut his glories in
> When Christ the mighty maker died
> For man the creature's sin

Outside the range of human observation, God was on center stage. Like a prism, the cross reflects the beauty of God. Here for all to see, God was redeeming sinners while remaining perfectly sinless. God picked us up from the gutter without defiling Himself. Since we offended an Infinite Being, an infinite sacrifice had to be made for us. Only God could do that. As Pascal says, "The incarnation shows man the greatness of his misery by the greatness of the remedy which he required."

Now if someone accuses God of associating with sinners,

the reply is that believing sinners have been declared as righteous as Christ. God sees them legally through the perfections of Christ. These fallen beings owe God not one whit of righteousness, for Christ has paid it all.

In California a man was given a speeding ticket. After the judge gave the sentence, he left the bench to stand with the defendant and pay his fine. It does not matter how high God's standard is just as long as He meets it for us. And until we know how bad we are, we will never know how good God is!

This God, the God of Christianity, is different from the gods of other religions. As I've already pointed out, Allah, the tribal God of Mohammed, is not a trinity and therefore could never be incarnated. Since there are many gods in eastern religions, they cannot claim exclusivity, nor can any one of them promise their adherents the gift of forgiveness and personal reconciliation with the Religious Ultimate. No other religion lays claim to an exclusive, creator God who becomes a man to redeem humanity.

In fact, Buddhism could survive without Buddha; when Buddha was asked how he would like to be remembered, he answered that his followers should not trouble themselves with that question since only his teaching really mattered. The teachings of Hinduism could survive regardless of who originated them. Even Islam could survive if the revelations had come through some other prophet. Neither of these leaders claimed to personally have the ability to rid the human heart of sin. But Christianity could not have survived without Christ, the second person of the Trinity coming to earth and dying on the cross. His mission was redemption, and that was not accomplished by His teaching but by His death. To empty the Cross of its meaning is to strip it of its power.

The idea that God Himself would suffer and provide a sacrifice to reconcile and forgive mankind is unique to Christianity. No other religion says that the best of human effort and teachings cannot save us. A rescue mission had to be undertaken that involved both a method of forgiveness and the creative power to change our basic human disposition. Only a personal God acting intentionally could do that.

God Alone Can Offer Salvation as a Gift

If you have followed the argument so far, you'll agree that logic requires that salvation must be offered as a gift to fallen mankind. A gift can only be refused or accepted; it cannot be earned. This gift is not given indiscriminately, but only to those who believe. That is, it is given to those who despair of saving themselves, those who depend on Christ alone.

"For by grace you have been saved through faith; and that not of yourselves, it is the gift of God; not as a result of works, that no one should boast" (Ephesians 2:8–9). If we ask why God requires faith, it is because He appreciates being believed. Faith is not itself a meritorious act; the merit is in the One to whom it is directed. It is a gift given to those to whom God would show His mercy. Faith does not set out to earn God's favor but depends solely on the undeserved favor of God.

I've met people who think that they have sinned too much or too long to be reconciled to God. What they need to understand is that this gift is available to anyone no matter how great his sin. It is much better to be a good citizen than to be a criminal, but if a generous man wished to give the same gift to both, that is his prerogative. Since neither man earns it, the extent of their personal sins and failures is, from this standpoint, irrelevant.

Just as the driest plot of ground is in the greatest need of rain, so those who are great sinners are often the first to realize that they have a need only God can meet. And just as the earth makes no contribution when the rain comes, but benefits from the gift, so we benefit from the righteousness we do not deserve. Remember the words of Christ, "I am not come to call the righteous, but sinners to repentance" (Matthew 9:13 KJV).

God does all the giving, we do all the receiving. Our contribution is to admit our sins and our helplessness. God's contribution is to give us Christ's righteousness and make us members of God's family forever.

Christ taught that those who accept this gift are few in comparison to those who either deliberately reject it or ignore the offer. To admit that only Christ can save us is difficult. When we receive this gift, we revise our own estimate of ourselves downward. That makes the gift difficult to accept.

God Alone Guarantees Salvation

Once the gift is received, can it be returned? Some think that we can lose our salvation through backsliding or rebellion. But when God bridges that infinite chasm and makes a fallen member of the human race His child, the process cannot be undone.

Too much is at stake for God to lose a child who now belongs to Him. Just as I do not disown my children when they are disobedient, so God is committed to us for now and eternity. We are sealed with the Holy Spirit until the day of redemption (Ephesians 4:30).

To put it differently: What would you think of a shepherd who was given one hundred sheep in the morning and returned in the evening with ninety-two? He would be ridiculed for his carelessness, weakness, and failure to carry out his basic responsibilities. Often sheep do go astray, and others follow false paths made by robbers who seek to lure them from the flock. But a competent shepherd knows these things. He keeps a watchful eye on each sheep; and when it strays, he brings it back by hook or crook.

Christ assured us that He is a competent shepherd. "My sheep hear My voice, and I know them, and they follow Me; and I give eternal life to them, and they shall never perish; and no one shall snatch them out of My hand. My Father, who has given them to Me, is greater than all; and no one is able to snatch them out of the Father's hand" (John 10:27–29). Elsewhere He taught, "And this is the will of Him who sent Me, that of all that He has given Me I lose nothing, but raise it up on the last day" (John 6:39).

This gift, once given, is ours forever.

God Alone Gives Us the Assurance of Our Salvation

In Michelangelo's painting of the final judgment, the expressions on the faces of those about to be judged reflect uncertainty and fear. No one in the fresco, except the virgin Mary, knows his or her fate. Perhaps this depicts Michelangelo's own apprehension about death, or the prevailing belief that no one could have the assurance in this life that he will be gladly welcomed by God into heavenly bliss.

Is it possible for us to know that we have been acquitted before God so that a blessed eternity is assured? All non-Christian religions (and even those branches of Christendom that make works a part of salvation) insist that the answer is no. The reason is obvious: As long as human merit contributes to the salvation process, not one of us can know that we have done enough to earn our way.

Some have gone so far as to assert that those who claim to have assurance that they will go to heaven at death are guilty of the sin of presumption. Of course they are right, given the premise that salvation is a cooperative effort between us and God. Even if 95 percent of the salvation process were done by God and 5 percent were up to me, assurance would be beyond reach. We could never be sure that we have done our part of the bargain.

New Testament Christianity asserts that we can have personal assurance because all our requirements are met by Christ who has impeccable credentials. When Augustine realized that God's standards were too high for him to meet, he cried out, "O, God, demand what you will, but supply what you demand!" He understood that we do not have to fear God's high standard as long as He meets it for us. That is precisely the good news of the gospel.

Yes, we can have assurance about our relationship with God. As mentioned above, Christ said that His sheep heard His voice; there is a bond of ownership formed based on both objective and subjective data. John the apostle wrote, "These things I have written to you who believe in the name of the Son of God, in order that you may know that you have eternal life" (1 John 5:13). Surely God who has given us a detailed revelation would not leave us in doubt about the most important question we could possibly ponder. We're talking about damnation or glory, hell or heaven.

Three witnesses help us know where we stand. The first is the promises of Christ who said that those who believed on Him would have eternal life (see, for example, John 3:36; 5:24). To believe means "to rely upon" or "to trust." Such faith is a confession of our own helplessness, with a conscious decision to rely on Christ, the Redeemer.

Saving faith may at times doubt, but it continues to look to Christ, confident that He will do exactly as He promised. The initial faith with which a person believes grows in the lives of those who have been made members of God's family. We must trust neither our own works, nor baptism, nor other sacraments. The amount of faith is not as important as the object of faith, namely, Christ and His perfect work on the Cross.

The second witness is the Holy Spirit. "The Spirit Himself bears witness with our spirit that we are children of God" (Romans 8:16). The Holy Spirit not only regenerates us as we turn to Christ in faith, but He indwells us. A personal sense of the Spirit's presence is God's gift to those who are members of His family. An inner certainty arises within the human heart.

Third, there is the fruit of a new life, the works that result from the new birth, a miracle done by God in the human heart. Two of the most obvious changes are a love for Christ and His Word along with a new perspective on sin. We now see sin for the impurity that it really is, and the need to maintain fellowship with our heavenly Father becomes a priority. God changes our inner disposition so we have a new spiritual appetite with a desire to know the God who has saved us.

God Alone Gives Us a Future with Him

Christianity does not teach reincarnation but resurrection (1 Corinthians 15). This respect for the human body contradicts the Gnostic claim that matter is evil. And it contradicts the Eastern claim that we lose our individuality in a cycle of rebirths. Our disintegrated bodies will be reconstituted so that we will have an eternal body. Our souls (the mind with its memories and affections) will be rejoined to our bodies so that we shall be whole people, personally in fellowship with other people and God forever. Eternity is neither vague nor shadowy, but individual, conscious, and eternal. Despite receiving new indestructible bodies and a new nature, we will be the people we are now for all eternity.

Now we can better understand why Christianity stands alone, unable to be combined with other gods, other prophets or theories of salvation. The strength of the gospel is in its purity; whenever we add, we subtract; whenever we combine, we dilute.

THE RIGHT SAVIOR?

Many false cults claim Christ as their Savior but deny His deity. But a Christ who isn't quite God would be like a bridge broken at the farthest end. Such a Christ cannot even begin to build a bridge to span the infinite chasm that separates us from God. A counterfeit Savior always results in a counterfeit salvation.

Christ Jesus of Nazareth predicted that people would be deceived because they would accept pseudosaviors, that is, those who make startling claims for themselves but in the end fail to deliver on their promises. He also predicted that these Christs would promote their credentials with various signs and wonders and that a gullible generation will believe. We can't just believe in any Christ, we must have faith in the right one.

What shall we make of folk singer Arlo Guthrie who says he had an experience with Jesus Christ on his back porch? He says, "I know I sound crazy when I talk about this . . . and it's really difficult to put into words because no words can describe it. There was this bright light and everything was known about me, and it was just total love. I was just free to be what I was."[6]

Guthrie led a discussion at the Parliament of the World's Religions on the topic, "Towards a Civilization with a Heart." He arrived with his guru Ma Jaya Bhagavatie of the Kashi Ashram that draws from a mixture of Hinduism, Christianity, Buddhism, and Judaism. All this is part of the spiritual path he started on seventeen years ago when he had a vision of Jesus.

The apostle Paul attributed a belief in such Christs to the direct work of Satan. "For such men are false apostles, deceitful workers, disguising themselves as apostles of Christ. And no wonder, for even Satan disguises himself as an angel of light. Therefore it is not surprising if his servants also disguise themselves as servants of righteousness; whose ends shall be according to their deeds" (2 Corinthians 11:13–15).

Satan will appear in whatever form he is expected to come. If you are Catholic, he will come as Mary or one of the saints; if you are a Protestant, he will appear as Christ, with a message of love. If you are a Hindu, he will appear as Krishna. He will make the bait as attractive and friendly as he can. His motive, of course, is to get people to believe in a Christ who is not able to save.

Martin Luther often struggled with doubt and with the devil. He was well aware of how easily we as human beings are deceived because of the experience of St. Martin, the figure in church history after whom Martin Luther was named. The story goes that St. Martin had a vision of Christ. But when he glanced at His hands to make sure it had nail prints, the apparition disappeared. So he never knew whether he had encountered Christ or the devil!

When a new prophet arises and claims to be a further revelation from God; when someone tells you that you should transcend Christianity and link up with the cosmic Christ, I strongly suggest you look for nail prints.

Only Christ, Jesus of Nazareth, will pass the test.

NOTES

1. Ron Rhodes, *The Counterfeit Christ of the New Age Movement* (Grand Rapids: Baker, 1990), 15.
2. Ibid., 27–56.
3. *Christian Research Journal,* Summer, 1989, 12.
4. Ibid., 13.
5. Douglas Groothuis, "The Shamanized Jesus," *Christianity Today,* 29 April 1991, 31.
6. *Chicago Tribune,* 14 September 1993.

AN EXTRAORDINARY RESURRECTION—

Could the Disciples Have Made Up the Story?

An atheist, Antony Flew, uses a parable told by John Wisdom to illustrate what he thinks is the lack of evidence for the existence of God.

> Once upon a time two explorers came upon a clearing in the jungle in which there were both flowers and weeds. One explorer says, "Some gardener must tend this plot." The other disagrees, insisting that there is no gardener. So they pitch their tents and set a watch. No gardener is ever seen.
> But the believer insists that there is an invisible gardener. So they set up a barbed wire fence, electrify it and patrol it with bloodhounds, reasoning that even an invisible man could be smelled though he could not be seen. But the fence is never tripped and the bloodhounds never cry out. No matter how long the explorers keep their vigil, no gardener is ever detected.
> Yet the believer is unconvinced. He insists, "But there is a gardener, an invisible, intangible, elusive gardener; a gardener insensible to electric shocks, who has no scent and makes no sound, a gardener who comes secretly to look after the garden which he loves."
> But the skeptic despairs, "Just how does what you call an invisible, intangible, eternally elusive gardener differ from an imaginary gardener, or even from no gardener at all?"[1]

Flew makes two points. First, there is no evidence for an invisible, intangible, elusive God who tends the world. He has never been seen nor can He be detected with the latest scientific equipment. This world, like an unkept garden, has both weeds and flowers; both evil and good. There is, says Flew, no reason to believe that someone tends the plot.

Second, Flew says believers are unwilling to allow any evidence to count against their faith. They refuse to stipulate the conditions under which they would surrender their belief; nothing is allowed to count against it. Flew asks us, "What would have to happen before you were to disbelieve in the existence and love of God?" If nothing will count against your faith, it proves you have given it a privileged position immune from proof or disproof. Such a belief, he says, which is compatible with anything and everything, is meaningless.

Every religion has the responsibility of responding to Flew's challenge. We have every right to ask a Buddhist, Hindu, or Muslim: What would have to happen before you would give up your belief? What evidence would you accept that would count decisively against your creed? We cannot give our religious convictions a privileged position that is closed to rational investigation, or else we have to relegate our beliefs to private opinions and personal preferences. Unless we can point to evidence outside ourselves, evidence accessible to everyone, we have no reason to say that our beliefs are true for us and for others.

Only the historic Christian faith can meet Flew's challenge. We believe that there is evidence that God actually entered into His garden; His footprints have been seen on this planet.

Our faith is not compatible with virtually anything. We are willing to state conditions under which we will surrender our faith: If the Resurrection of Christ can be proved to be a hoax, I for one will cease believing in Christ.

You'd think that Paul was thinking of Antony Flew when he wrote:

> For I delivered to you as of first importance what I also received, that Christ died for our sins according to the Scriptures, and that He was buried, and that He was raised on the third day according to the Scriptures, and that He appeared to Cephas, then to the twelve. After that He appeared to more than five hundred brethren at one time, most of whom remain

until now, but some have fallen asleep; then He appeared to James, then to all the apostles; and last of all, as it were to one untimely born, He appeared to me also. . . . But if there is no resurrection of the dead, not even Christ has been raised; and if Christ has not been raised, then our preaching is vain, your faith also is vain . . . and if Christ has not been raised, your faith is worthless; you are still in your sins. (1 Corinthians 15:3–8; 13, 14, 17)

Paul is strident in his argument: A man who claimed to be God was put to death and was raised to prove that His claims were valid. And if it be proven that Christ is still dead, if the grave still contains His body, we will stop preaching and humbly admit we have been misled. Our faith is not compatible with anything and everything, but is based on reliable historical events.

Why is the physical resurrection of Christ so important to our faith? First, it fulfills His prediction that this is the final sign He would give to the world (Matthew 12:39–40; 16:21). Reason requires that if Christ is God, He could not stay in the tomb indefinitely.

Second, this is proof of our own final resurrection. Strictly speaking, Christ is the only person in history who was resurrected. Lazarus was simply resuscitated; he had to die again. Christ was resurrected with a new, indestructible body, a prototype of the body we shall receive.

What compelling reasons do we have that Christ has in fact been raised from the dead? Let us evaluate the evidence according to accepted standards of historical research.

THE DOCUMENTS ARE RELIABLE

Let's suppose you don't believe the New Testament to be the Word of God; suppose you choose to study it with the same objectivity and healthy skepticism used in evaluating any other ancient documents. How would the New Testament compare with other ancient literature in reliability and accuracy?

Three tests used to judge ancient documents[2] are:

Bibliographical Test

This test answers the question: Can we arrive at a stable, reliable textual foundation for the claims set out in the gospel records? To be more precise: None of the original documents of the New Testament are in existence today. That, of course, is true of all ancient writings; in each case we must be satisfied with copies of copies. So, the question is: Do we have reliable copies of the original documents?

What do we make of the gap that exists between the original writings and the copies? In the case of the New Testament we have excellent evidence that the copies are for all practical purposes identical with the originals.

First, the gap is relatively short in comparison to other writings. For Euripides the interval is 1,600 years, for Plato it is 1,300 years, and for Demosthenes it is as low as 1,200 years. Despite these many centuries, we believe we have accurate texts about ancient history and philosophy because ancient copyists took great pride in reproducing such writings. However, in the case of the New Testament the interval is 250 or 300 years, a relatively short period by comparison.

Second, and most important, we can close the gap even further. In recent decades, numerous papyri manuscripts have been found in Egypt which confirm that the New Testament documents were already in existence in the first century. Listen to the words of Sir Frederic Kenyon, who at one time was the Director and Principal Librarian of the British Museum, "The interval then between the dates of original composition and the earliest extant [existing] evidence becomes so small as to be in fact negligible, and the last foundation for any doubt that the Scriptures have come down to us substantially as they were written had now been removed. Both the authenticity and the general integrity of the books of the New Testament may be regarded as finally established."[3]

We have reason to believe that the textual tradition is indeed reliable. The New Testament manuscripts presently in existence have essentially the same content as the originals.

Internal Evidence

This test answers the question: Are the writers consistent and factual? Do they give evidence of believability? Here we must, as historians, give the writers the benefit of the doubt unless they disqualify themselves by inconsistencies and errors. In the case of the gospel writers, they claim to be eyewitnesses, giving vivid details that could only be known by those who were present at the events.

Consider the claims of Luke, who received much of his information from Peter. He pointed out that there were many who wrote eyewitness accounts about the life and ministry of Christ and added, "It seemed fitting for me as well, having investigated everything carefully from the beginning, to write it out for you in consecutive order, most excellent Theophilus; so that you might know the exact truth about the things you have been taught" (1:3–4).

How accurate was Luke as an historian? Sir William Ramsey, after years of painstaking archaeological and geographical investigation of Luke's writings (Luke was also the author of Acts), concluded, "Luke's history is unsurpassed in respect of its trustworthiness."[4]

Examples of detailed historical reporting are found in all of the gospel writers. Remarkably, all four of them—Matthew, Mark, Luke, and John—despite their different perspectives agree on their portrait of Christ. They give us no reason to discredit their accounts.

External Evidence

This test answers the question: Do other historical materials confirm or deny the internal testimony provided by the documents themselves? Here we consult the insights of archaeology and history. Many books have been written on these topics, of course, and almost all the data confirms the trustworthiness not just of the New Testament but of the Old as well.

Archaeology itself is not an exact science and therefore its interpretations sometimes change. For example, when I studied in Israel in 1968, an archaeological team from an American college concluded that Joshua was wrong in his report about the Battle at Ai. Their evidence, they said, contradicted the way the city had been captured. Yet other archaeologists interpreted the same data in a different light; some even insisted that the students were digging at the wrong site! Sometimes archaeology has cast doubt on the Bible but has later confirmed its accuracy. A few years ago *Time* magazine had an article entitled: "Score One For The Bible."[5] It reported that Joshua's description of the collapse of the walls of Jericho had now been confirmed by fresh archaeological investigation. In my opinion, the headline should have read: "Score One for the Archaeologists!"

Christians, of course, do not believe that the reliability of the Bible is dependent on each new archaeological discovery. We are quite convinced that the ancient eyewitness accounts are more reliable than investigations thousands of years removed from the events. Nevertheless, we are gratified that serious historical/archaeological studies have shown that the Bible is trustworthy and available for close scrutiny.

There are numerous references to Christ in secular literature, including an account of Christ's resurrection in the writings of Josephus. These texts put the New Testament accounts into a broader context and give independent evidence to the existence and career of Christ.[6]

Why can we believe in the Resurrection? We are confident that we have a reliable text that corresponds to the original documents. In a previous generation liberal scholars tried to show that the New Testament was written in the second century, far removed from the events themselves. But few hold to these theories today because the evidence points to first-century documents that have come down to us substantially as they were written.

But of course the question arises: How do we know that the eyewitnesses themselves were credible? Could Christ's followers have created the stories about Him?

THE EYEWITNESSES ARE CREDIBLE

Granted that the documents which are in existence closely mirror the originals, we still must face a nagging question: Is it possible that the disciples of Christ made up the stories about

Him? Maybe the man Jesus lived, and His zealous followers portrayed Him as a miracle-man, a man whom they so admired that they embellished everything He did, attributing amazing words and works to Him. Could they have taken a man and made him their Messiah, their God?

Skeptics have argued that the first century was one in which the nation was gripped with "messianic fever." The Jews were impatient with Roman domination and eager to find a man who could be their Messiah. Indeed, there are several accounts of men who claimed to be messiahs, but their predictions and actions ended in disappointment. Jesus, in the hands of skillful storytellers, somehow managed to survive in the minds of many as a Messiah/Savior.

But there are several powerful reasons why the disciples would not have taken a man, even a remarkable man, and made Him into a Messiah. They were morally and spiritually incapable of putting divine words in His mouth and attributing divine works to His hands. Why?

1. *Christ would have been disqualified as a candidate for Messiahship.*

He contradicted virtually all Jewish messianic expectations at the time. According to S. W. Baron, the Zealots expected the redeemer to appear sword in hand and lead the people against Rome's military power. Others expected a cosmic cataclysm out of which would arise a new world with the chosen people marching to final salvation. Many believed the Messiah would bring back the remnants of the Ten Tribes and reunite Israel and Judah. As John Warwick Montgomery says, "The single fact that official Jewry crucified Jesus for blasphemy is sufficient ground for rejecting the idea that Jesus fulfilled the messianic dreams of His time."[7]

Millar Burrows, who did extensive work on the Dead Sea Scrolls, wrote, "Jesus was so unlike what all Jews expected the son of David to be that his own disciples found it almost impossible to connect the idea of the Messiah with him."[8]

No one was expecting a messiah who would have the audacity to unite Jews and Gentiles as children of one heavenly

Father. Taking down of the middle wall of partition and in effect abolishing the law—such ideas were never even thought of, much less associated with the Messiah. As the great Jewish scholar Edersheim said, "Assuredly, the most unlike thing to Christ were His times."[9]

2. *The disciples would not have deified a mere man.*

Even if Christ had met the messianic expectations of the day, no devout Jew would have been psychologically, ethically, and religiously capable of taking a man and calling him God. The disciples were steeped in the Judaistic teachings of the unity of God, "Hear O Israel, the Lord our God is one Lord." Would they have conspired to the gravest form of blasphemy by taking a man and making him God, thereby deliberately breaking the first commandment, "Thou shalt have no other gods before Me"?

The followers of Christ were practical, ordinary fisherman and tax gatherers who were not given to extravagance and pipe dreams. They concluded Christ was the Messiah not because they were overcome with messianic fever, but because they were persuaded by the evidence.

3. *The disciples were transformed by the Christ they came to know.*

Far from creating Him, they changed from a frightened group of men to a fearless band who were willing to give their lives for their Master. Christ had predicted that He would be crucified and then rise from the dead as a final proof of His deity. Let's consider the story itself:

> Then some of the scribes and Pharisees answered Him saying, "Teacher, we want to see a sign from You." But He answered and said to them, "An evil and adulterous generation craves for a sign; and yet no sign shall be given to it but the sign of Jonah the prophet; for just as Jonah was three days and three nights in the belly of the sea monster, so shall the Son of Man be three days and three nights in the heart of the earth." (Matthew 12:38–40)

Aware of this prediction, Pilate specified that guards were to be stationed at the tomb to prevent the disciples from stealing His body, then claiming that He had arisen. However, according to the documents, Christ did rise, eat with the disciples, and appear to more than 500 people over a forty-day period.

Only such evidence can account for the existence of the Christian church, the transformation of a Jewish community into a committed group of followers powerful enough to triumph over the paganism of Rome. A dead Christ would have bred a dead faith; only a living Christ could have transformed an unlikely band of men into an army whose weapons were the Good News of the Gospel of Christ.

THE ALTERNATIVES ARE UNBELIEVABLE

Of course some people are unhappy about the Resurrection. As mentioned, Pilate conspired with the chief priests and Pharisees to keep Christ in the tomb. For fear that someone might come and steal the body and claim a resurrection, Pilate gave orders, "You have a guard; go, make it as secure as you know how" (Matthew 27:65). And along with a guard, they rolled a stone over the mouth of the cave to make sure it was sealed. But evidently they did not make it secure enough, for on the first day of the week the stone was rolled away and the tomb was empty.

Alternative theories have been suggested to account for the empty tomb. Some have said that Jesus only fainted on the cross and the cool tomb revived Him. But the Roman soldiers made sure that a man was dead before he was taken from a cross. Also, it is improbable that a wounded victim would have been able to push the heavy stone away and elude the guards. And would such a bruised, dazed teacher be able to inspire His disciples to die for Him?

Others said that Christ's enemies stole His body, but the body would have been produced by them to stifle the disciples' preaching on the Resurrection. Against all credulity, some have said the disciples did steal the body to fake a resurrection. But would they have been willing to die for a Christ they knew was dead?

We do well to listen to the words of J. V. Langmead Casserley in his 1951 lectures at King's College, London. He said that the attempts to explain away the empty tomb demonstrate that "the assertion of the Resurrection is like a knife pointed at the throat of the irreligious man, and an irreligious man whose religion is threatened will fight for his own creation, his most precious possession, like a tigress fighting for her cubs."[10] Enough said.

Many men who have greatly influenced Western civilization have simply assumed that Christ was irrelevant to their grandiose ideas. In effect, they have tried to keep Christ sealed in the tomb; they propagated their theories and for the most part, ignored Him. We can say that, symbolically, one stone after another has been rolled in front of Christ's tomb in a vain attempt to keep Him dead—out of sight, out of mind.

The skeptic, David Hume, referred to in an earlier chapter, thought his essay on miracles would disprove the Resurrection. He argued: We have uniform experience against miracles, and there can be no exceptions to this rule! But his basic premise assumes the conclusion. How can he know that we have "uniform experience" against miracles? Obviously if a resurrection has occurred, we do not have "uniform experience" against such a miracle! Our responsibility is not to pontificate about what can or cannot happen in the world, but simply to look at the evidence to see what has in fact happened. There can be no philosophical argument which keeps Christ in the tomb.

Hume was a philosopher (the word means, "lover of wisdom") but unfortunately he didn't believe the words of Colossians 2:3 which say of Christ, "In whom are hidden all the treasures of wisdom and knowledge." How, we might ask, can Christ be kept in the tomb by philosophy when He is king of philosophy?

Karl Marx took the stone of economics and rolled it in front of the tomb, hoping to keep Christ out of sight. He was reared in the Rhineland of Germany and baptized a Lutheran. But with his friend Engles he later wrote the *Communist Manifesto*, then *Das Kapital*. He said that religion was the opiate of the people, and that within time these myths would be exterminated.

But he didn't do very well in keeping Christ in the tomb. Today, countries that officially adopted Marxism are turning to

Christianity with growing faith in a resurrected Savior. How could Christ be kept out of economics and politics when His shoulders bear the governments of the world? "For a child will be born to us, a son will be given to us; And the government will rest on His shoulders . . ." (Isaiah 9:6).

Sigmund Freud rolled the stone of psychotherapy in front of the tomb to keep Christ at arm's length. He claimed that our idea of God was a figment of our imagination, an idea we create to give us hope. Driven by aggression, our sex drives, and a strong desire for a father image, we create God. He believed that psychoanalysis would be the answer to the distressed human spirit.

Today, psychiatry itself is on the couch; there are many conflicting theories of what works and what doesn't, and the entire discipline is in disarray. Too bad that Freud didn't understand that Christ is the master of the human soul. He knows the most minute details of all men, has the power to forgive their sins and restore them to God. How could Freud ever think he could dispense with Christ who is the "Wonderful Counselor, the Mighty God"?

Voltaire took the stone of culture and rolled it in front of Christ's tomb. He had good reason to be critical of the church of his day; but in rejecting Christ's so-called followers, unfortunately he also rejected Christ. He predicted that in less than one hundred years the Bible would be a forgotten book. Yet, I'm told that the house in which he lived was later purchased by the Geneva Bible Society so the Bible could be spread throughout Europe! Voltaire evidently forgot that Christ is the king of culture; He is the lily of the valley, the bright and morning star.

Darwin took the stone of science and rolled it in front of Christ's tomb. Though he himself professed belief in God, he thought that evolution could explain the origin of life, and the next generation of scientists building on shaky evidence said that God was an unnecessary hypothesis. Yet today evolution is crumbling. Overwhelming evidence is accumulating that it is simply impossible to believe that life began with blind chance. Dr. Paul Leman, the editor of the French Encyclopedia, said candidly, "Evolution is a fairy tale for adults."

How could Darwin have mistakenly ignored Christ about whom we read, "For by Him all things were created, both in the heavens and on earth, visible and invisible, whether thrones or dominions or rulers or authorities—all things have been created by Him and for Him" (Colossians 1:16).

How unthinkable that science could keep the king of science in the tomb!

Kingdoms come and kingdoms go, but Christ lives. Centuries come and centuries go, but Christ lives; kings are crowned and kings are uncrowned, but Christ lives; emperors decree Christ's extinction, but Christ lives; skeptics mock and skeptics die, but Christ lives.

Perhaps you are rolling a stone of your own making in front of Christ's tomb, hoping to keep Him at a safe distance. Anger, rebellion, pride, or religious prejudice—all of these have been used to shy away from the full implications of Christ and His claims. But remember, just as you cannot take the water in the oceans of the world and confine it in an eye dropper, so you cannot keep the living Christ dead.

The fact of Christ's resurrection gives us hope as we face death, not because we are blind to death's horrors, but because we look with confidence upon Jesus of Nazareth. The Resurrection is the Great Reversal, the one reality which gives us the assurance that no other realities of our existence need ever permanently discourage us. "The resurrection," Tozer said, "demonstrates once and for all who won and who lost."

EVEN A SKEPTIC BELIEVED THE EVIDENCE

"Doubting Thomas," as the disciple is frequently called, reminds us that Christ is accommodating to skeptics whose hearts are open to embrace the truth but who sincerely believe there is not enough evidence. Doubt is not unbelief; unbelief is usually rebellion against evidence. Doubt, someone has said, "is stumbling over a stone we do not understand. Unbelief is kicking at a stone we understand all too well." It has been said that those who have never doubted have never truly believed.

Thomas had a streak of pessimism, a hunch that in the end nothing would ever come out quite right. When Christ told His disciples that it was time to return to Jerusalem, Thomas said to his friends, "Let us also go, that we may die with Him" (John 11:16). He was a loyal pessimist, the kind who would describe a cup as half empty rather than half full.

After the Resurrection, Christ appeared to His disciples in the Upper Room, but Thomas was absent. Like most melancholics he likely preferred to suffer alone.

Iron! Wood! Blood! As far as Thomas was concerned it was all over; he had witnessed a tragic end to a beautiful life.

Was he justified in his doubt? There are some good reasons why he should have believed in the resurrection of Christ.

First, Christ had predicted that He would die and be raised. What is more, He took the time to explain this in detail to His disciples (Matthew 16:21). The miracles of Christ should have given Thomas the confidence that the grand miracle of the Resurrection was not only possible but necessary. This was one life that could not end on a cross.

Second, he should have believed because of the report of the disciples. When they saw him they all shouted, "We have seen the Lord!" This would have been a lawyer's dream—ten testimonies and they all agree! But such evidence was not enough for this pessimist. The prediction of Christ and the word of His friends lacked the credibility of a personal encounter.

Thomas is not the kind of disciple who was so gripped with "messianic fever" that he was seeking for reasons to make Christ into God. Like the other disciples, he was a hard-headed fisherman who was only willing to believe if the evidence was "beyond reasonable doubt."

Christ let eight days go by, eight days to let Thomas brood over his sense of loss and hopelessness. Then Christ accommodated Himself to Thomas's stipulations:

> The other disciples therefore were saying to him, "We have seen the Lord!" But he said to them, "Unless I shall see in His hands the imprint of the nails, and put my finger into the place of the nails, and put my hand into His side, I will not

believe." And after eight days again His disciples were inside, and Thomas with them. Jesus came, the doors having been shut, and stood in their midst, and said, "Peace be with you." Then He said to Thomas, "Reach here your finger, and see My hands; and reach here your hand, and put it into My side; and be not unbelieving, but believing." Thomas answered and said to Him, "My Lord and my God!" (John 20:25–28)

Face! Body! Scars! This was his Master, the Christ.

Why did Thomas believe? He had a willingness to believe; he was an honest doubter. He didn't say, "I dare you to convince me!" No, he made some stipulations, and when they were met, he believed. He was not a gullible fisherman, but he was honest enough to admit that the evidence was convincing.

He also displayed a personal faith. "My Lord, and My God!" he exclaimed. He knew that a Christ who could rise from the dead was one to whom we owe our allegiance.

Is the evidence for Christ's resurrection just as obvious as $2 + 2 = 4$? No, it cannot be, for mathematics is simply the joining of two concepts in the mind. Nor is it like science whose experiments can be repeated. The evidence for the Resurrection is rooted in proper historical investigation; it is based on accepted rules of manuscript evidence. The evidence is enough for the honest doubter, but not enough for the dishonest one.

Your name just might be in the Bible. When speaking to Thomas, Christ added, "Because you have seen Me, have you believed? Blessed are they who did not see, and yet believed" (v. 29). We could paraphrase, "blessed are you—Tom, Ruth, or Marie—because though you have not seen, yet you have believed!"

A Buddhist in Africa who was converted to Christianity was asked why he changed religions. He replied, "It's like this: If you were walking along and came to a fork in the road and two men were there and one was dead and the other was alive, which man's directions would you follow?"

Our faith is open to investigation. We do not give religious truth a privileged position, immune from rational evidence. There are good reasons to believe that God has entered the garden.

We are invited to trust the Gardener.

NOTES

1. Antony Flew, "Theology and Falsification" in *New Essays in Philosophical Theology* (New York: Macmillan, 1955), 96.

2. John Warwick Montgomery, *History and Christianity* (Downer's Grove: InterVarsity, 1971). This book demonstrates that the New Testament is reliable in that it passes the tests by which documents are evaluated.

3. Quoted in Montgomery, 28.

4. Ibid., 32.

5. *Time,* 5 March 1990.

6. Josh McDowell and Bill Wilson, *He Walked Among Us* (San Bernardino: Here's Life Publishers, 1988), 35–70.

7. Montgomery, *History,* 69.

8. Ibid., 71.

9. Ibid., 68.

10. Ibid., 77, 78.

AN
EXTRAORDINARY
ASCENSION—

What Is Christ Doing Today?

Science has made wondrous strides in past decades. The explorations into the heavens and the discovery of the secrets of the atom have contributed to a virtual explosion of knowledge. But there are some frontiers science cannot penetrate; there is a veil through which it cannot pass. For example, scientific experiments cannot prove or disprove whether the human soul continues after death or, if it continues, the kind of existence it enjoys (or endures). Yes, there are some clues that the soul is separable from the body, such as near death experiences, but these are subject to a variety of interpretations. To be near death might not be the same as being actually dead. We'd like to enter that different realm, make our observations, and return with a report. That, of course, is not possible.

Given the curtain that divides us from the hereafter, it is not surprising that the sacred writings of virtually all the leading religions are silent about the present responsibilities of their dead leaders. The most devout Muslim will admit that he really does not know what Mohammed has been doing during these many centuries, though he is believed to be in paradise; Hindus can only guess what role Krishna plays on the other side of the grave. The same goes for the followers of Bahá ú lláh, Zoroaster, and others. Not only is the present existence of these leaders unclear, but so are their plans for the future.

Christ, as we have learned, claimed to be God in the flesh and was raised from the dead to confirm His words. He is the only qualified person to tell us what lies on the other side of death. Given these credentials, we should not be surprised that we not only have details about His bodily Ascension into heaven, but a description of what He is doing today and what His plans are for tomorrow. He is a leader who is now consciously in charge and will rule over the affairs of this world even more directly in the future. But I'm ahead of the story.

We should not be surprised that a Christ who was raised from the dead has also ascended into heaven. Let's read Luke's account:

> And after He had said these things, He was lifted up while they were looking on, and a cloud received Him out of their sight. And as they were gazing intently into the sky while He was departing, behold, two men in white clothing stood beside them; and they also said, "Men of Galilee, why do you stand looking into the sky? This Jesus, who has been taken up from you into heaven, will come in just the same way as you have watched Him go into heaven." (Acts 1:9–11)

Christ went up, that is, His body actually left the earth and moved confidently toward the sky. Then once He entered the atmospheric heavens, He disappeared in a cloud. He took a journey that involved space and time; His body did not vanish, it moved upward from the Mount of Olives until it disappeared beyond human sight. He actually "passed through the heavens" (Hebrews 4:14).

This event has been ridiculed because, we are told, it is contrary to a modern scientific understanding of the universe. The ancients believed in a three-leveled universe, with heaven above, the flat earth in the middle, and hell below. Since Copernicus, we know that the earth is round and therefore what is an upward movement in the Middle East would be a downward movement, in, say, New Zealand. Or to state the objection differently, to the people on the other side of the world Christ's Ascension would have been a "descension" of sorts into regions unknown.

In reply we must remember that the Bible describes heaven as both a *place* and a *state.* As a place, it is the very dwelling place of God; it could be far beyond the stellar universe. Biblically, we know that there are three heavens: (1) the atmosphere, (2) the stellar universe, and (3) the abode of angels, the dwelling place of God. When Paul says Christ passed "far above the heavens" (Ephesians 4:10), he wants us to grasp as best we can the awesome position Christ now holds. Where that is, we do not know; for all we know, after a cloud received Him, He may not have continued to travel in a straight line. We must be satisfied to know that He went to the central dwelling place of the Almighty.

As a state, heaven represents an entirely different order of reality. Its occupants can apparently traverse great distances in an instant, unhindered by the spatial limitations that curtail our travel plans. At the Ascension, Jesus went from one mode of existence to another; from the material world to the spiritual world, from the finite world to the infinite world. We don't know the coordinates of heaven, but we can say, thanks to eyewitnesses, that He left this earth gradually, visibly, and bodily.

The arrival of Christ in heaven changed the character of heaven forever. This is the first time perfect humanity entered the presence of God. He was the first man in heaven with a resurrected body. When the believers of the Old Testament died, their bodies went to the grave, and their souls either went to Sheol, as some believe, or to heaven. Either way, they do not yet have their permanent resurrected bodies, for the resurrection of the dead is yet future. (Enoch and Elijah had unusual disappearances; it would, however, be strange indeed if, contrary to all others, they already have their resurrection bodies.)

Of this we can be certain: Never before had Christ been in heaven joined to a human body. Never before had there been a man with nail prints at the center of the universe. Christ had resided in heaven before, but not as the God-man. On earth He had prayed to His Father, "glorify Me on earth with the glory which I had with Thee before the world was." Now He had returned to a direct display of that former glory. Today Christ in perfect manhood is in the midst of the throne seated in the heavens. His glory is like that on the Mount of Transfiguration; He is ablaze with blinding light.

At His arrival the angels were most likely confounded. They had studied God's plan of redemption and were astounded at His wonder, love, and power. They had pondered God's descent to sinful humanity; yet, considered in another way, they saw His humiliation as a visual demonstration of God's indescribable love and grace. In fact, there would not have been an ascent if there had not first been a descent that accomplished the divine purpose. Yes, Christ had occupied this exalted position before, but the Ascension was proof that He had accomplished His mission; the Ascension, in the words of F. B. Meyer, "set an eternal seal upon the victory won in the mystery and darkness of the descent." Now that He had returned as man, they assuredly sang, "Holy, Holy is the Lord God of Hosts, earth and heaven are filled with His glory!"

Even before His death Christ had, in effect, told the disciples that the Son of Man would ascend (John 6:62). The Ascension was a necessary confirmation of His successful mission on earth. Augustine said, "for unless the Savior had ascended to heaven, his nativity would have come to nothing. . . . His passion would have borne no fruit for us and His most holy resurrection would have been useless."

This arrival in heaven signified that Christ had the following rights:

THE RIGHT TO OWNERSHIP

When the God-man stepped back into the glories of heaven, no one questioned His right to enter. He did not come pleading for mercy. No mediator opened the door for Him. He was not receiving a privilege that was beyond His rights. He was victoriously returning home after a painful but successful journey.

Why did He own this honor?

First, because of *who He is.* The presence of His human body does not obscure His divine nature. Let us remember that He is the one who created the heavens. "For by Him all things were created, both in the heavens and on earth, visible and invisible, whether thrones or dominions or rulers or authorities—all things have been created by Him and for Him" (Colossians 1:16). The earth was created *by* Him and *for* Him! The heavens were created *by* Him and *for* Him! The angels who attend His every move were created *by* Him and *for* Him! No wonder He didn't merely enter heaven but strode into it as its rightful owner and heir.

What does Paul mean when he says Christ ascended to "fill all things"? It may simply mean that He fills all things by His presence, His sovereignty, His activity. We are told by some that the universe is infinite, but logically we have to say that Christ (Jehovah) is greater than the universe. The creation could never be as great as the Creator. He "upholds all things by the word of His power" (Hebrews 1:3). His exaltation to this position of prominence was therefore a return to the glory He had before creation, the glory He enjoyed before Bethlehem. He returned to the position that was His eternal right.

Second, He had a right to heaven because of what He *had done.* He had carried out the responsibility which He and the Father had agreed He would do in eternity past. The night before He was betrayed, He had told His Father, "I glorified Thee on the earth, having accomplished the work which Thou has given Me to do" (John 17:4). And what was that work? "When He had made purification of sins, He sat down at the right hand of the Majesty on high; having become as much better than the angels, as He has inherited a more excellent name than they" (Hebrews 1:3b–4).

As God, Christ was perfect, yet we are told "He learned obedience from the things which He suffered. And having been made perfect, He became to all those who obey Him the source of eternal salvation" (Hebrews 5:8–9). At His new arrival in heaven, He was not simply perfect as the Son of God, but also perfect as the Son of Man. He was perfect in the delicate task of assuming human nature, overcoming temptations, facing unmentionable humiliation and pain, and finally passing through the gates of death and then (thankfully) resurrection.

Christ had a *natural* right to return to His rule in heaven as God, but now He also had an *earned* right to enter heaven as man. He had accomplished a work on earth that represented God's most remarkable ingenuity and grace.

Previously He could be called *Creator;* now He could also be called *Savior.* Previously He could rule from heaven by virtue of who He was; now He could rule because of the tests He had endured. Previously He could crush Satan with raw power; now He proved He could crush him by rescuing men from every tribe and nation out from under his evil authority. Previously He could reign as God; now He could reign as man. Above the heavens is one who was forever there, but now He is there as man as well as God.

Christ now resides in the place that He owns. Appropriately, the book of Revelation places Christ "in the midst of the throne." As the hymn writer, Thomas Kelly, put it:

> The head that once was crowned with thorns
> Is crowned with glory now
> A royal diadem adorns
> The mighty Victor's brow
>
> The highest place that heaven affords
> Is his, is his by right
> The King of kings and Lord of lords
> And heaven's eternal light.

Surely heaven fell silent with breathless wonder. God the Son had arrived with the sure knowledge that a mission had been accomplished. Psalm 24 was used by Israel in a procession during a major festival. As the worshipers walked up the hill of Zion they sang:

> Lift up your heads, O gates, and be lifted up, O ancient doors, that the King of glory may come in! Who is the King of glory? The Lord strong and mighty, the Lord mighty in battle. Lift up your heads, O gates, and lift them up, O ancient doors, that the King of glory may come in! Who is this King of glory? The Lord of hosts, He is the King of glory. (vv. 7–10)

Understandably, the early church related this psalm to Jesus as He ascended into the heavenly temple. He changed heaven after He arrived and left earth in a different condition than He found it. The arrival of the king makes every head turn in adoring wonder.

THE RIGHT TO HEADSHIP

Christ arrived in heaven as the head of a whole new race. The firstborn Son had begotten many sons through His work on the Cross. "For whom He foreknew, He also predestined to become conformed to the image of His Son, that He might be the firstborn among many brethren" (Romans 8:29). These sons whom He brought into glory (you and I) are now a part of the church of which He is the head.

What is the purpose of this headship? Paul says that God "seated Him at His right hand in the heavenly places, far above all rule and authority and power and dominion, and every name that is named, not only in this age, but also in the one to come. And He put all things in subjection under His feet, and gave Him as head over all things to the church, which is His body, the fulness of Him who fills all in all" (Ephesians 1:20–23).

As head, Christ fulfills important responsibilities:

He Strengthens Us

He shares His life. We are not expected to walk through this life in our own strength: "from whom the entire body, being supplied and held together by the joints and ligaments, grows with a growth which is from God" (Colossians 2:19). Just how are we connected to Christ? Through the gift of the Holy Spirit which was given to His people after the Ascension. "Therefore having been exalted to the right hand of God, and having received from the Father the promise of the Holy Spirit, He has poured forth this which you both see and hear" (Acts 2:33).

We share Christ's life, just like the head shares the same life as the rest of the body. And since the head has gone on before, the members will surely follow.

He Unites Us

Those who are joined to Christ are connected to each other. By the Holy Spirit we grow together until the body is complete: "but speaking the truth in love, we are to grow up in all aspects into Him, who is the head, even Christ" (Ephesians 4:15). We show our loyalty to His headship when we obey all of His commands, especially the command that we love one another. There is a unity that transcends denominational commitments.

He Represents Us

Christ entered into the heavenly sanctuary not just as conqueror, but also to assume the role of High Priest. "Since then we have a great high priest who has passed through the heavens, Jesus the Son of God, let us hold fast our confession. For we do not have a high priest who cannot sympathize with our weaknesses, but one who has been tempted in all things as we are, yet without sin" (Hebrews 4:14–15).

Paul taught that Christ's presence at God's right hand undercut Satan's right to accuse us, "Who will bring a charge against God's elect? God is the one who justifies; who is the one who condemns? Christ Jesus is He who died, yes, rather who was raised, who is at the right hand of God, *who also intercedes for us*" (Romans 8:33–34; italics added).

Does Christ actually pray to the Father in our behalf? Perhaps. But His very presence as our representative at the right hand of God assures us that we stand fully received in the Father's presence. In the words of Charles Wesley:

> Five bleeding wounds He bears,
> Received on Calvary;
> They pour effectual prayers,
> They strongly plead for me;
> "Forgive him, O, forgive," they cry,
> "Nor let that ransomed sinner die!"

He Is with Us

Let's not think of Christ as so far removed that He is only remotely affected by our personal pain and struggles. The opposite is the case: He taught His disciples that it is better that He go away so that the Comforter would be sent who would abide with us forever. True, His body can only be in one place at one time, but by His Spirit He is constantly with His people. He stands with us in our need.

To remind yourself of the nearness of Christ, think of Him as standing next to you in the room, riding in the car or walking with you as you go to work. (What TV programs might we not watch if Christ sat on the couch with us?)

Yes, we should think of His resurrected physical body as being in heaven, but even in body He might be nearer to us than we can ever think. Heaven might seem far away, but that is simply because of our concept of distance. With God, millions of miles are reduced to milliseconds; the concept of distance as a limitation vanishes. G. Campbell Morgan, thinking of the soldiers in World War II, wrote, "He can most certainly, suddenly, gloriously appear upon the field of battle to a dying soul."

Apparently Christ sometimes leaves His seat to stand at the Father's right hand. When angry men were preparing to stone Stephen, even before the stones began to fly, we read, "But being full of the Holy Spirit, he gazed intently into heaven and saw the glory of God, and Jesus standing at the right hand of God; and he said, 'Behold, I see the heavens opened up and the Son of Man standing at the right hand of God'" (Acts 7:55–56).

Christ was not too busy to take note of one of His servants who was about to experience the pain of martyrdom. Whatever else may have been happening on the planet at that moment, Stephen had Christ's full attention. Our trials never escape His notice; the heavenly circuits are never overloaded.

When Saul persecuted believers, killing some and putting others in jail, Christ physically appeared to him en route to Damascus. Christ's question not only caught Saul's attention, but also put to rest the idea that in heaven Christ might just be too preoccupied to be aware of our personal needs. The question was, "Saul, Saul, why are you persecuting Me?" (Acts 9:4). When His people hurt, Christ hurt. When they felt alienated and rejected, He felt likewise. He is "touched with the feelings of our infirmities."

If we ask how Christ as man can keep track of all that is happening in the lives of millions of believers simultaneously, we must appeal to His deity. What a man cannot do, the God-man can. Remember His Spirit pervades the whole universe. Speaking of our High Priest, the author of Hebrews writes, "And there is no creature hidden from His sight, but all things are open and laid bare to the eyes of Him with whom we have to do" (Hebrews 4:13).

As the head of the church, Christ is not about to neglect His duties. His Ascension is a sign of His headship.

His triumphant arrival in heaven also signified his Kingship. He arrived as the undisputed ruler of the universe.

THE RIGHT TO KINGSHIP

Paul described Christ as ascending "far above all rule and authority and power and dominion, and every name that is named, not only in this age, but also in the one to come . . ." (Ephesians 1:21). We read that Christ "passed through the heavens."

The point of these passages is not one of *distance,* but *dominion;* it is not *travel,* but *triumph.* Christ is not just above any other name (or any other god) in space, but He is above them in power, authority, and victory. However neglected He might have been at the Parliament of the World's Religions, Christ stands without a serious rival in the universe.

En route to heaven Christ might well have been beset with the concentrated opposition of Satan and all of his hosts; passing through the atmosphere "the prince of the power of the air" would have launched another of his many desperate but fruitless attacks against the Son of God. Christ sustained these without any hint of failing, for His victory had already been accomplished.

Think of this: Christ will never increase in strength, for He already is omnipotent; He will never increase His knowledge, for already He is omniscient; He will never be given a larger kingdom, for already He is omnipresent. He is not waiting to be crowned King, but He is waiting to be *recognized* as King. Everything and everyone is already under His feet. Such a Ruler is certainly worthy of our recognition, adoration, and obedience. What a privilege to let Him win our hearts!

His Present Rule

Look at the world and you would never guess it was being ruled by an omnipotent king. How do we reconcile a world that is out of control morally and spiritually with the leadership of a king who has all power and authority? We must be patient with those who question Christ's performance, for it does not appear as if He is bringing order out of chaos.

If Christ does not lack for power, love, and authority, why does He not bring an evil world to its senses? The best argument for atheism is the apparent indifference of God to human misery. We can forgive the skeptics for asking whether the King of the Universe is doing His job. If He does not lack for power, does He lack the mercy that would put an end to this madness? Does He care?

Crime is escalating out of control. Wars are destroying whole countries. Women are being raped; children are being abused. In some parts of the world famine is killing thousands of people every day. In our own country, marriages are being torn apart, drugs are destroying children. Who can comprehend the terror, the fear, and the buckets of tears shed every hour on this hapless planet? Why would a king allow His kingdom to be overtaken by rebels?

We must distinguish two aspects to Christ's rule. Today He rules from heaven, exercising divine *restraint.* Indeed, multiplied millions do not even acknowledge His existence, much less do they own Him as king. Daily He is insulted, either because of neglect or misrepresentation, or classified as simply one among many. This is what happens today, but tomorrow it will be different.

Christ is waiting, "but He, having offered one sacrifice for sins for all time, sat down at the right hand of God, waiting from that time onward until His enemies be made a footstool for His feet" (Hebrews 10:12–13). Today He is waiting, biding His time until He will come to exercise His right as King in the presence of all men. His present rule from heaven is one of divine restraint.

Why does He wait? He is letting history prove a point—namely, that man cannot rule the world. He has delegated His rule to the kings and princes of this world, letting them exercise their authority as they see fit. Of course their influence is limited by the divine will and purpose, so we can confidently say that God's will is being done on earth. History is marching toward a goal.

His Future Rule

The wait ends when Christ returns to the Mount of Olives in splendor and glory. Then He will take direct control, subduing His enemies and bringing the world to justice. Then He will fulfill the ancient prophecy, "And He will judge between the nations, and will render decisions for many peoples; And they will hammer their swords into plowshares, and their spears into pruning hooks. Nation will not lift up sword against nation, and never again will they learn war" (Isaiah 2:4).

The present and future aspects of Christ's rule can be seen by putting these two passages together: On the one hand Paul says that God has already "put all things in subjection under His feet" (Ephesians 1:22); on the other hand He speaks of it as a future event: "then comes the end, when He delivers up the kingdom to the God and Father, when He has abolished all rule and all authority and power. For He must reign until He has put all His enemies under His feet" (1 Corinthians 15:24–25).

If every name that is named is already under Christ's feet, why must He wait until every enemy is finally brought under His subjection? As I explained, Christ is a king in waiting; He is a man who has been crowned in heaven but not yet acknowledged as king on earth. *His coronation by God has been relatively private; the recognition of it on planet earth will be very public indeed.*

Be clear about this: *Christ is just as much a king when He is waiting as when He is winning!* He is just as much king in His ascent as He will be at His descent. He is just as much in control in heaven as He will be on earth. For now He is content to direct the affairs of planet earth through erring representatives; He is willing to let Satan roam the earth like a criminal who has skipped bail. For now the rebels have taken over the premises. But the day will come when the only king whom God recognizes will be acknowledged by every tongue ever created, "Therefore also God highly exalted Him, and bestowed on Him the name which is above every name, that at the name of Jesus every knee should bow, of those who are in heaven, and on earth, and under the earth, and that every tongue should confess that Jesus Christ is Lord, to the glory of God the Father" (Philippians 2:9–11).

Today some subjects welcome the reign of the king, but for the most part, the drama is played out in defiance of His authority. But at the curtain call the King will appear. The saga will end so differently from how it all began.

WHAT DOES THIS MEAN TO ME?

Believe it or not, Christ's Ascension has a meaning similar for us as it was for Him. Just as God raised Christ up, so we have been raised up with Him: "and raised us up with Him, and seated us with Him in the heavenly places, in Christ Jesus" (Ephesians 2:6). Think of how we benefit. The same privileges, with the exception of headship, apply for the believer.

Ownership

You and I as believers are already in heaven, heirs to an incredible inheritance. Christ promised that He would prepare a place for us: There is a crown that only you can wear, a mansion that only you can enter. Peter said there is a place "reserved in heaven for you." The only way I can be cast out of heaven is if Christ Himself is thrown out! He is representing me, protecting my interests.

Kingship

What Christ has by divine right was purchased for us by divine mercy! We will never become what He is, but we shall enjoy what He has. We stand amazed at the wonder of God's grace. "And there shall no longer be any night; and they shall not have need of the light of a lamp nor the light of the sun, because the Lord God shall illumine them; and they shall reign forever and ever" (Revelation 22:5). William Cowper, the eighteenth century poet troubled by bouts of deep depression, wrote,

> How thou canst think so well of me
> And be the God thou art
> Is darkness to my intellect
> But sunshine to my heart

Christianity is often faulted because of its teaching on the depravity of mankind, the fact that we cannot do a single work that will merit the approval of God. Although no other religion insists on our utter sinfulness, none lifts us to greater heights of saintliness. Christ takes us from the *mud* and invites us to walk on *marble;* He takes us from the *pit* and invites us to walk in the *palace.* No other religion brings us so *low* and exalts us so *high.*

Savonarola gained fame as a preacher in Florence, predicting that a flood of judgment would come upon the city if it did not repent. He attacked the lax, corrupt citizens through fiery preaching and censorship. During the carnival in 1496 he orchestrated "the bonfire of the vanities" a ceremony where people brought their gambling artifacts, lewd books, and cosmetics to be burned.

He was excommunicated for refusing to stop preaching against the pope, and later he was tried for heresy and executed.

Despite the reversals he experienced, and though the truth did not triumph in his day, before his death he said, "He who believes that Christ rules above, need not fear what happens below!"

Malcolm Muggeridge said, "All news is old news happening to new people." There is nothing happening in the world that is news to God; it is all old news known from before the foundation of the world. Christ reigns in heaven today, fully in charge of our fallen world. And although we do not yet see all things under His feet, that day is coming closer. Those who believe that He reigns from the heaven need not fear what happens on earth.

Let the King be on His way!

AN
EXTRAORDINARY
RETURN—

Which God Reigns?

At this point, you might be thinking, "If Christ is supreme, if He is Lord and King, why doesn't He prove it?" The Bible predicts that He will prove it decisively and with finality. The last battle in history as we know it will settle the one important question: Which God reigns?

Let's do our best to understand how the pluralism of our day might eventually grow to become a worldwide movement. At the head of this coalition will be a charismatic leader who will mesmerize the nations with his brilliance and ingenuity. This religious/political ruler will embody everything that our age stands for, but in the end he will be destroyed by Christ.

To sketch the portrait of this leader, let us begin in the Hofberg Library in Vienna, Austria, where there is a spear believed by many to be the one used to pierce the side of Christ. One day when Adolph Hitler was in his early twenties, he overheard a tour guide describe the spear for a group of guests, "This spear is shrouded in mystery; whoever unlocks its secrets will rule the world." Later Hitler said that those words changed his whole life.

Hitler, you will recall, spent four years of his life in Vienna, earning money by drawing sketches. He spent all his free time in the Hofberg Library, reading books on history and the occult.

He became an expert in Eastern religions and was known to purchase such books in used book stores, and then resell them so he could buy more.

After hearing the comment about the mystery of that spear, Hitler became fascinated with it. He read all he could about its history, trying to determine whether it could indeed be traced back to the time of Christ. He became convinced that this one did have awesome powers for good or evil. He traced it back to the time of Constantine and believed that the emperor had it in hand when he conquered Rome in A.D. 314.

In all, Hitler believed that forty-five Roman emperors or kings had used this spear. He noted that when they had it in their possession, they were victorious; when it fell out of their sphere of ownership, their empire crumbled, sometimes in a single day. Though it is doubtful that this was the spear used to pierce Christ's side, for Hitler it was a point of contact for Luciferic transformation.

According to Ravenscroft in his book *The Spear of Destiny,* young Hitler was mesmerized by this object. He would stand staring at it for hours, inviting its hidden powers to invade his soul. He felt as though he himself had held it in his hands in an earlier century. He was bewitched by its mysteries and power. One witness said that when Hitler was transfixed before it, he was engulfed in "ectoplasmic light."[1]

When he left Vienna to go to Munich, he soon surrounded himself with those who were dedicated to the pursuit of occult experiences and phenomena. The original members of the National Socialist Party (dubbed the Nazis) were hard-core Satanists who introduced him to deeper levels of "spiritual perception."

Chief mentor to Hitler was Dietrich Eckart who, through the rituals of black magic, enabled Hitler to be transformed into a totally demonized being. Eckart claimed that he had received a satanic annunciation and that he was destined to prepare the vessel of the Antichrist, the man who would be inspired by Lucifer to conquer the world and lead the Aryan race to glory.[2]

Hitler assumed the uncontested leadership of the Nazi party in 1921, the year he celebrated his thirtieth birthday. He was now ready for his official career. A friend wrote that Hitler was "possessed by forces outside of himself . . . of which the individual Hitler was only the temporary vehicle." His satanic control was so complete that many saw his body as only the shell for the spirit who inhabited him. His speeches mesmerized tens of thousands and made them fully committed to the Nazi cause.

After he conquered Vienna without a shot, he entered the Hofberg and took the spear from behind the glass and clutched it to his bosom for the first time. It became for him a spear of revelation. "It was," he says, "as though I were holding the whole world in my hands." It became for him one of many bridges to occult powers. According to Ravenscroft, this spear was taken to Nuremberg under heavy guard; and through a fluke of mistaken identity, it fell into the hands of Americans on the day Hitler committed suicide in his bunker in Berlin.[3]

Hitler, I believe, is a prototype of the Antichrist. After World War I, Germany was in a state of hyperinflation, thus most Germans had their savings wiped out in a matter of days. Hitler appeared to be a political genius who brought them out of economic chaos. He was a man who initially gave a sense of pride and identity to the German people who needed their faith in humanity revived.

Antichrist, I believe, will walk onto the stage of history and do economic and political miracles. He will capture the imagination of millions, or rather billions, who will follow his peace and prosperity platform. With smooth words and reasonable assurances of good intent, he will lure an unsuspecting world into the greatest bloodbath that has ever taken place on planet earth.

The world is so interdependent that instability in any sector will spread and destabilize all societies. With the world in a state of unrest the Antichrist will seize power.

Satan does not know when Christ is planning to return to earth. He knows *what* will happen, but he doesn't know *when*, so he must always have someone in place to play the role of Antichrist should the need arise. Author Reinhold Kerstan, who witnessed Hitler's dramatic rise to power, says that this generation is open to "an updated Fuehrer."

The final battle in history as we know it will be between two religious powers. On the one hand will be all the religions of the world unified and directed by Antichrist; on the other side of the conflict will be Jesus of Nazareth and His followers. Here, at last, the truth will be revealed for all to see.

Millions are already believing in the very doctrines Antichrist will proclaim. The Parliament of the World's Religions emphasized the very doctrines that will eventually be accepted by the vast majority of the world's population.

THE DOCTRINES OF ANTICHRIST

Let's review the doctrines of Antichrist and then describe how the final religious confrontation will end. Look around you and you will agree that these ideas are already widely accepted.

Self-Transformation

Marilyn Ferguson in her book *The Aquarian Conspiracy* writes that an "irrevocable shift" is overtaking us. It is not a new system but a new mind. An underground movement is changing society based on an "enlarged concept of human potential . . . a transformation of personal consciousness."[4]

The New Agers teach, and Antichrist will concur, that we can change ourselves by using the proper techniques. The human mind has latent powers which, if properly trained, can tap into the spiritual powers of the universe. Man is in a period of evolutionary transition that is so great that we are leaving an Old Era for the New Era. There are two ways to bring about such a transformation; the slow way is through meditation; the accelerated track is psychedelic drugs.

Hitler preferred the speedier route. Already in Vienna, he befriended a used book dealer, Ernst Pretzsche, who introduced him to a drug which produced clairvoyant visions and heightened spiritual perceptions. This drug contained mescaline and had the power to lead Hitler into a "fruitful experience of transcendent consciousness." In this way he was empowered to perform deeds which he believed fate decreed.

Rauschning wrote, "Hatred is like wine to him, it intoxicates him . . . he would have men against whom he had a grudge tortured to death in the most horrible way. He had the instincts of a sadist finding sexual excitement in torturing others."[5]

Thus was Hitler thoroughly changed into a tool of Satan. The Antichrist of the Bible will experience a comparable transformation. Daniel predicted that he would be a king who would be skilled in intrigue, "And his power will be mighty, but not by his own power, and . . . he will destroy mighty men and the holy people" (8:24). In Revelation we repeatedly read that his authority and power were not natural to him, but rather these were "given to him" (13:7).

Satan evidently indwells this man, taking total possession of his every word and movement. This transformation of consciousness is Satan's most dazzling deception. He wants not only Antichrist but all humans to have a "demonic new birth" that corresponds to Christ's teaching, "you must be born again." Think of the delight he receives when people have an encounter with him and think it is an experience with the living God!

The Deity of Mankind

The apostle Paul calls Antichrist the son of destruction, "who opposes and exalts himself above every so-called god or object of worship, so that he takes his seat in the temple of God, displaying himself as being God" (2 Thessalonians 2:4).

All of us recall Shirley MacLaine shouting, "I'm God! I'm God!" as she ran along the beach in her TV miniseries of several years ago (Charles Colson said, "Aren't you glad she's wrong!"). Irrational as it may seem, mankind is ready to believe that we are gods, the ground of our own consciousness.

Ever since Satan told Eve that if she accepted his suggestion she would "be like God, knowing good and evil," the idea of the divinity of man has always been popular in occult teaching. This brazen notion is man's attempt to mimic Satan's rebellious desire to be like the Most High. This absurdity has always been widely believed in the East, but now it is gaining acceptance in the Western world as well.

By the time Antichrist appears, the world will be ready to deify a leader if he appears to have what it takes to unite the world and bring in the new era of peace. But the missiles of war will fly behind the doves of peace.

The world will gladly trust this new Caesar. At the beginning of the tribulation period, he will make a covenant with Israel, evidently guaranteeing the peaceful existence of that small but significant country. After three and one-half years, he has enough confidence to go to Jerusalem and break his treaty. He enters the temple which will have been built at that time and desecrates it, declaring himself to be God. Although such a pronouncement may be reprehensible to the Jews, the world at large will welcome the opportunity to worship a man. If we are all little gods, why cannot Antichrist be the embodiment of God? He will be accepted as the Messiah of the world.

It is not enough for Satan to inhabit a man who will claim to be God. The master deceiver will actually try to duplicate the three members of the Trinity! These three personalities will do their best to confuse the world by pretending to be the true and living God.

Let's take a better look at this unholy triad.

a. Satan corresponds to God the Father, and he is spoken of in Revelation as the dragon who gives his authority to the beast who is Antichrist (Revelation 13:4).

b. The Antichrist, who is empowered by the dragon, corresponds to Jesus Christ. He will try his best to do miracles and duplicate something similar to Christ's resurrection. Speaking of this beast, John writes: "And I saw one of his heads as if it had been slain, and his fatal wound was healed. And the whole earth was amazed and followed after the beast" (Revelation 13:3).

The world will believe that the Antichrist survived a wound that would have put any other man to death. The skeptical will be convinced that this is the man to follow and worship.

Finally, there will be religious unity. The dragon and the beast will receive the worship of the world.

And they worshiped the dragon, because he gave his authority to the beast; and they worshiped the beast, saying, "Who is like the beast, and who is able to wage war with him?" And there was given to him a mouth speaking arrogant words and blasphemies; and authority to act for forty-two months was given to him. And he opened his mouth in blasphemies against God, to blaspheme His name and His tabernacle, that is, those who dwell in heaven. And it was given to him to make war with the saints and to overcome them; and authority over every tribe and people and tongue and nation was given to him. And all who dwell in the earth will worship him, everyone whose name has not been written from the foundation of the world in the book of life of the Lamb who has been slain. (Revelation 13:4–8)

All who dwell upon the face of the earth will worship him! One notable exception will be the elect whose names were written in the Book of Life from before the foundation of the world. Apart from the relatively few who have the courage to oppose this dictator, he will capture the hearts of everyone. During the apex of Hitler's career in Germany, the Lord's prayer was changed by many to read, "Our Father Adolph who art on earth, Hallowed be thy name, the third Reich come . . ." Antichrist will welcome such worship.

c. The third member of the unholy trinity is referred to as the second beast in Revelation 13:11–18. Just as the Holy Spirit draws attention to Christ, so the assignment of this evil man is to get the world to worship Antichrist, "And he makes the earth and those who dwell in it to worship the first beast, whose fatal wound was healed" (v. 12). To gain their confidence, he performs great miracles, even causing fire to come down out of heaven to the earth. He also gives breath to an image, giving the appearance of being able to create life.

How will Antichrist gain such religious power? He will do some things that people think only God can do. Paul says of him that he will be "in accord with the activity of Satan, with all power and signs and false wonders, and with all the deception of wickedness for those who perish, because they did not receive the love of the truth so as to be saved" (2 Thessalonians 2:9–10). The three words used here—*power, signs, and wonders*

—are all used for the miracles of Christ. Antichrist's power to duplicate the works of Christ is so remarkable that multitudes believe!

Many of the miracles performed by the unholy triad are specified: Fire will come down from heaven, an image will be made to speak (possibly this will be accomplished through trickery since it is unlikely that Satan can create life), and the fatal wound will be healed (Revelation 13).

A world schooled in New Age thought will believe.

A Commitment to Globalism

Antichrist will be firmly committed to globalism, the belief that the massive problems in the world can only be solved by bringing all nations under one banner. Through economic, political, and religious reform, we can put an end to hunger and war.

At the Parliament of the World's Religions, "A Global Ethic" was adopted that stressed the need for cooperation among the religions of the world to end hunger, war, and injustice. Much of the document could be supported by Christians, and yet at root it is stridently anti-Christian. For one thing, as pointed out earlier, the word *God* does not appear as a concession to Buddhists since many of them do not believe in the existence of any God or gods. Instead the word *earth* is capitalized throughout, reflecting the pantheistic emphasis of the conference. Second, the document is committed to the notion that we can personally experience a self-transformation and thereby the whole world can be changed. In keeping with this globalism, the final paragraphs contain these words:

> In conclusion we appeal to all the inhabitants of this planet. Earth cannot be changed for the better unless the consciousness of individuals is changed. We pledge to work for such transformation in individual and collective consciousness, for the awakening of our spiritual powers. . . . Together we can move mountains![6]

Traditional religions, therefore, must be viewed as a springboard to finding the hidden spirituality that is within all of us.

Whereas the old religions separated people into sharply divided camps, the new religion unites them under a common banner. Theology divides, the spirituality of self-transformation unites. In this new synthesis, religion and science are combined. God is defined as "energy" or "the force" that men can harness to bring about Utopia. The technology of advanced computers, lasers, and psychological control mechanisms will be at the disposal of the coming world dictator. Religion will be defined as the doctrine of the spiritual unity of mankind, and everyone will be forced to accept this or be tortured to death.

Antichrist will capitalize on the present doctrinal inclusiveness and bring about a religious unity that will encompass the globe. To quote John once more, "And all who dwell on the earth will worship him, everyone whose name has not been written from the foundation of the world in the book of life of the Lamb who has been slain" (Revelation 13:8).

A Commitment to Utopia

We've already emphasized that the rush to unite the religions of the world is driven by the belief that such unity will solve the problems of the world. Through the development of our human potential, we will usher in a New Era of Peace and Prosperity.

The Bible predicts that Antichrist will come to power as a peacemaker. "And through his shrewdness he will cause deceit to succeed by his influence; And he will magnify himself in his heart, And he will destroy many while they are at ease. He will even oppose the Prince of princes, but he will be broken without human agency" (Daniel 8:25).

The phrase, "he will destroy many while they are at ease" means that the Antichrist will take advantage of the peace movement. The King James Version translates this phrase, "Through peace he shall destroy many." Peace will be his platform; peace will be his bait. The world will be at rest militarily, and there will be a worldwide feeling that at last the nations of the earth can destroy their weapons. But this false sense of security will only prove to be an advantage to the coming prince.

Since the Middle East still is an explosive powder keg, Antichrist will make a covenant with the tiny nation of Israel to guarantee its survival. With much worldwide fanfare the covenant is signed and the world breaths more easily. Peace is at hand.

Plans to eradicate hunger and the disproportionate economic balance of the world will fall quickly into place. Health care and education will be high on the agenda of world leaders, driven by the persistent belief that it is time to seize the day in an atmosphere of unrestrained euphoria. Man, we will be told, is in the process of evolutionary change, and the future is now.

But while the leaders publicly speak peace, privately preparations for war will escalate. Science will give the world hideous new chemical weapons and new methods of torture such as have never been seen before.

An Intolerance of Dissent

Presently, a document like "A Global Ethic" has no power; no one has to sign an agreement that he or she is willing to fall in line with the global agenda. Its goal was to be inclusive enough to be supported by all religions. But if some do not get on board, how will unity eventually be enforced?

Initially, people who do not sign on will be branded as warmongers who are unconcerned about the problems of the world; they are prejudiced, selfishly opinionated. But when Antichrist comes to power, he will use economic reprisals against those who do not follow his program. Those who cooperate will be given a mark on the forehead or on the hand, and they will be permitted to buy and sell; those who refuse will be tortured. Primarily, two groups will be singled out for persecution—the Christians and the Jews.

New Age literature speaks of a purging that must take place so that the New Era is not delayed. This will involve bloodshed and suffering so negative emotional energy can be dissipated. Some writers speak candidly of Christians as the cancerous tissue that must be cut out for the healing of planet earth. Author Moira Timms says that the plagues of the book of

Revelation are reserved for those who stand in the way of the coming new order:

> . . . the plagues of Revelation are a special package of Karma visited upon the obstinate that they might awaken to their wrong attitudes . . . animals that don't adapt become extinct. Remember? Survival today means understanding and responding to change within the context of the "internal revolution."[7]

Modern technology will give the Antichrist control over most of the people in the world. There will be the use of lasers and computers for surveillance and possibly new biochips that can be inserted into the human brain to make a person believe in any false doctrine. Refined methods of torture will be routinely used.

The mark on the hand or forehead might be a computer chip which could usher in a new era of a cashless society. Scanners in stores, factories, and banks would be used for all business transactions. Perhaps the number given to an individual would not even be known by that individual, thus no one could ever get his PIN (Personal Identification Number) even at gunpoint.

Erwin Chargaff, the "Father of Bioengineering," wrote that he perceives there is a new barbarism in our future:

> I see the beginnings of a new barbarism . . . which tomorrow will be called a "new culture." . . . Nazism was a primitive, brutal and absurd expression of it. But it was a first draft of the so-called scientific or pre-scientific morality that is being prepared for us in the radiant future.[8]

Just think of the awe and worship that would be accorded a man if he were to arise on the stage of history claiming to be the reincarnation of Winston Churchill or John Kennedy! With some spectacular miracles to prove it, he will be enthusiastically accepted as the Savior of the World.

After a few years of successful economic and military maneuvers, he will go into the temple of God in Jerusalem to claim his official title to deity. He will break his covenant with Israel and desecrate the temple. Then he will begin the cruelest reign of terror known to man.

Even though I believe that the Christians who are living today will be raptured before the Great Tribulation, the fact is that the persecution I've spoken about can begin at any time. Even in our day, freedom of speech is being restricted if it does not fall in line with the liberal agenda. Thankfully, all of this shall come to a dramatic and permanent end.

THE BATTLE OF ARMAGEDDON

Just as Antichrist grasps for ultimate control, his kingdom will unravel. For one thing, God begins to heap judgment on the world; for another, Antichrist's European coalition begins to fall apart. Some countries break for their own independence.

Eventually four confederations of nations gather in the Middle East for the Battle of Armageddon. At last, truth is about to triumph. Here are some of the characteristics of this coming conflict.

It Will Be Fought in Israel

This battle will not be limited to the plain of Megiddo in northern Israel. We know it will begin there, for we read, "And they gathered them together in the place which in Hebrew is called Har-Magedon" (Revelation 16:16). Eventually, the whole land of Israel will be engulfed in war and blood will be splattered as high as the horse's bridles for a distance of 200 miles (Revelation 14:20).

It Will Be the Worst Conflict in History

Christ said of those days, "For then there will be a great tribulation, such as has not occurred since the beginning of the world until now, nor ever shall" (Matthew 24:21). For sheer magnitude and cruelty, this war will be in a class by itself. The total depravity of the human heart will reach its fullest expression.

It Culminates in the Return of Christ

As the battleground is enlarged, two powerful armies vie for the rule of the world. This bloody battle is interrupted with a dramatic event that captures the attention of the world. Jesus Christ returns to the Mount of Olives with his saints in tow. Here is Zechariah's description:

> Then the Lord will go forth and fight against those nations, as when He fights on a day of battle. And in that day His feet will stand on the Mount of Olives, which is in front of Jerusalem on the east; and the Mount of Olives will be split in its middle from east to west by a very large valley, so that half of the mountain will move toward the north and the other half toward the south. (Zechariah 14:3–4)

Geologists tell us there is a fault line on the Mount of Olives that extends all the way down to the Dead Sea. When the feet of Christ step onto that mount, it will divide from east to west. The topography of the area will be remarkably changed.

Once Christ returns, the warring armies decide to drop their conflict and join what they consider to be a more important cause, namely to unite against Christ. Their hostility against God's Son, fueled by other so-called gods and inspired by Satan, will boil in fury. Here is one last opportunity to topple the Ruler of the Earth and throw His crown into the dirt.

Although the description of Christ's return is rather lengthy, it deserves to be quoted here:

> And I saw heaven opened; and behold, a white horse, and He who sat upon it is called Faithful and True; and in righteousness He judges and wages war. And His eyes are a flame of fire, and upon His head are many diadems; and He has a name written upon Him which no one knows except Himself. And He is clothed with a robe dipped in blood; and His name is called The Word of God. And the armies which are in heaven, clothed in fine linen, white and clean, were following Him on white horses. And from His mouth comes a sharp sword, so that with it He may smite the nations; and He will rule them with a rod of iron; and He treads the wine press of the fierce wrath of God, the Almighty. And on His robe and on His thigh He has a name written, "KING OF KINGS, AND LORD OF LORDS." (Revelation 19:11–16)

Who are those who accompany Him, "clothed in white linen, white and clean"? They are not angels but the saints who have just eaten at the Marriage Supper of the Lamb (v. 8). Since there is evidence that the believers on earth will already have been raptured before Antichrist assumes complete control, these are believers who have accepted Christ as Savior in this present age.

Catch your breath as you read this: We will follow Christ to subdue the nations of the earth in the final battle before the Millennial Kingdom. *All of us will stand with Him on the Mount of Olives and then march with Him to victory!*

All False gods Will Be Destroyed

Christ's would-be rivals will come to a humiliating and shameful end. They will finally be shown to be puppets of the god of this world. God will prove that no idol or group of idols pitted against Him will ever be able to take the credit for so much as a single answer to a single problem. The final days of Antichrist will be proof that only God can bring order out of chaos; only God can be just; only God can bring reconciliation and forgiveness. And only God's true Son can bring peace to the world!

Everyone will get to spend eternity with his or her god. Carefully read these two contrasting descriptions of eternity. I begin with a depiction of those who worshiped the beast and received his mark. We read:

> He also will drink of the wine of the wrath of God, which is mixed in full strength in the cup of His anger; and he will be tormented with fire and brimstone in the presence of the holy angels and in the presence of the Lamb. And the smoke of their torment goes up forever and ever; and they have no rest day and night, those who worship the beast and his image, and whoever receives the mark of his name. (Revelation 14:10–11)

After the glorious return of Christ to earth, there will be a period of peace that shall last for a thousand years. Christ will rule from Jerusalem, fulfilling the prophecies of the Old Testament. Satan will be bound for this period of time, but he will be loosed for a short while.

The horrid description continues:

> And the devil who deceived them was thrown into the lake of fire and brimstone, where the beast and the false prophet are also; and they will be tormented day and night forever and ever. (Revelation 20:10)

Notice that all three members of the unholy trinity are in the lake of fire. The beast (Antichrist) along with the false prophet (corresponding to the Holy Spirit) have already been there for a thousand years. But now the Dragon (Satan) is forced to join them. They along with all of their followers, both demons and men, are thrown into the lake of fire and tortured forever and ever. So the millions who took Antichrist's mark and the millions who followed other gods throughout the centuries will follow Satan, the beast, and the false prophet into the lake of fire. The great deceiver will have no satisfaction that he took so many with him, for his torment will only be that much greater. Every act of rebellion will be eternally and justly punished.

A startling contrast is portrayed of another kind of eternity:

> And I saw, as it were, a sea of glass mixed with fire, and those who had come off victorious from the beast and from his image and from the number of his name, standing on the sea of glass, holding harps of God. And they sang the song of Moses the bond-servant of God and the song of the Lamb, saying, "Great and marvelous are Thy works, O Lord God, the Almighty; Righteous and true are Thy ways, Thou King of the nations. Who will not fear, O Lord, and glorify Thy name? For Thou alone art holy; For all the nations will come and worship before Thee, For Thy righteous acts have been revealed." (Revelation 15:2–4)

Choose your God carefully. You will have to spend eternity with him (or her, if you prefer). It's not your sincerity that will count but whom you worship that will eternally matter.

Truth and Justice Will Triumph for All Eternity

There is a story about a boy who was reading a novel in the living room. His mother called to him, asking that he help with the dishes, "Mom, I can't come right now. The villain has the hero down and he's about to kill him. . . . I have to see how the story turns out!"

But as most mothers do, she persisted. So knowing that he had to go, he turned to the last page of the book and read it. There he discovered that the hero lived and the villain was killed. That afternoon as the boy walked into the kitchen he said, "That old villain . . . he's doing fine in chapter 5, but is he ever in for a shock when he gets to the last page!"

We are hurt but not disheartened by the fact that the Parliament of the World's Religions insulted Christ through neglect, misrepresentation, and classifying Him as one of the gods. This is the period during which rebellion is allowed to flourish; error appears to triumph, the King appears to be dethroned. But we have read the last chapter. Christ will triumph throughout all of eternity. And it is *eternity,* not *time,* that really counts.

That these things will happen is certain, the *time* is not. Blessed are those who are found waiting.

"Be on the alert then, for you do not know the day nor the hour" (Matthew 25:13).

NOTES

1. Trevor Ravenscroft, *The Spear of Destiny* (York Beach, Me.: Weiser, 1982), 64.
2. Ibid., 92
3. Ibid., 335–52.
4. Marilyn Ferguson, *The Aquarian Conspiracy* (Los Angeles: Jeremy P. Tarcher, 1980), 23.
5. Ravenscroft, *The Spear,* 176
6. "A Global Ethic," 1993 Parliament of the World's Religions, 9.
7. "Prophecies and Predictions: Everyone's Guide to the Coming Changes," 57–58.
8. Quoted in Texe Marrs, *Mega Forces* (Austin, Tex.: Living Faith, 1988), 24.

AN
EXTRAORDINARY
STUMBLING BLOCK—

Is Everyone Else Lost?

"You can't be serious!"

The man who spoke those words was not trying to be rude; he was just expressing surprise that I had the audacity to say that Christ was the only way to God. I knew that what I had said was, to put it mildly, out of step with our culture, but I was trying to help him understand that we have to play by God's rules, whether we like them or not.

We've all agonized over the implications of the fact that Christ stands alone among the religious leaders of the world. We wish the way to heaven were broader so that we could give a more acceptable reply to those who ridicule the Christian faith because, in their way of thinking, it does not take into account sincere worshipers in other religions. How do we answer those who accuse us of heartless narrow-mindedness? Or those who say that their God, thankfully, is more broadminded than ours?

At this point in the book, I can hear a whole chorus of objections:

— What about those who have never heard of Christ through no fault of their own? Are they excluded from God's grace?

— Is it fair for God to send anyone to hell, especially those who never had a chance to believe the message?

— Is it possible for sincere believers of other religions to be saved through Christ though they will not know Him until they get to heaven?

These are good questions and deserve answers, even if the answers are not what most of us would like to hear. Missionaries tell us that when people come to Christ they often ask, "What about our ancestors?" And as America becomes more diversified, as we become personally acquainted with those of other religions, the question of the salvation of sincere believers in other faiths is never far from our minds. In fact, the moment we argue for the uniqueness of Christ, we think of those who have never heard, or those who have heard of Christ but nevertheless sincerely follow another faith.

As the pressure of pluralism mounts, some evangelicals (those of us who hold to salvation through Christ alone) are rethinking these questions. Many are no longer content to give a simplistic answer but insist that the lostness of others must be reconsidered. Perhaps the traditional answer is not the right one.

So how shall we regard other religions? Are they primitive expressions of the true religion, or are they demonic, totally in opposition to the truth? And might not the sincerity of their devotees count for something in the day of judgment?

THE WIDER MERCY VIEW

Some would see other religions as friendly competitors who have much in common with Christianity and the work of the Logos (Christ) who enlightens every man that comes into the world. The religions are seen as having varying degrees of enlightenment, and when people come to Christ, they are given more light (the true light) which is but an extension of the flickering flame they have been following.

Clark Pinnock in his book, *A Wideness in God's Mercy,* and John Sanders in *No Other Name* insist that Christ is the only basis of salvation, but that it is not necessary to place direct faith in Him in order to benefit from His work on the Cross. God, the argument goes, knows that Christ is the only way of salvation, but those who have not heard the gospel are ignorant of this. Their own religion might function as a "schoolmaster" which unwittingly leads them to Christ.

Pinnock and Sanders would agree with Raymond Panikkar, that the "good and bona fide Hindu is saved by Christ and not by Hinduism, but it is through the sacraments of Hinduism, through the message of morality and the good life, through the mysterion that comes down to him through Hinduism that Christ saves the Hindus normally."[1] People can be saved *by Christ through the channel of other religions.*

Various suggestions have been made to explain how God brings the sincere devotees of other religions to salvation. First, there is the "later light" view. Some interpret 1 Peter 3:18, 19 (which says that Christ "went and preached to the spirits in prison," NIV) to mean that Christ went and preached the gospel to those who were in Hades. They conclude that people will get an opportunity to accept or reject Christ after death. In the early church, Irenaeus and Tertullian taught that Jesus delivered only the believers of the Old Testament from hell; Clement of Alexandria and Athanasius taught that Jesus delivered both Jews and Gentiles from hell and that this form of evangelism still continues today.

But there are serious objections to this view. For one thing, it is by no means certain that Peter taught that Christ went to Hades at all. An interpretation that is more in keeping with the context is that Noah, through the Holy Spirit in his day, "preached to the spirits which are *now* in prison." Also, even if Christ did preach in Hades, He may have simply announced victory to the inhabitants since there is no evidence that they were released from their abode. Finally, it is stretching the text to the breaking point to assume that Christ is doing the same today. Regardless of what interpretation we accept, it refers to an event that is past without the slightest hint that it continues today.

There is a second suggestion as to how God might save those who have never heard of Christ. God, it is said, will save others based on His foreknowledge. Since He knows not only what *has* happened but what *would have* happened under different circumstances, He would know whether someone who didn't hear the gospel in, say Sri Lanka, would have accepted it if he had been born in Canada. On this basis, the argument goes, He accepts them.

But even if election were based on foreknowledge (a view I don't accept), the idea that God saves some because of what would have been the case under different circumstances is wholly conjecture. Christ said that if the miracles He did had been done in Tyre and Sidon, "they would have repented long ago in sackcloth and ashes" (Matthew 11:21). Yet He gave no hint that this means that Tyre and Sidon will be saved in future judgment. We could all think of circumstances in which, to our mind at least, virtually anyone would accept Christ. But the Bible teaches that God takes into account what *has* happened rather than what *might* have happened.

Third, there are those who believe that God simply makes an exception and chooses to accept Christ's sacrifice in behalf of sincere individuals of other religions. In other words, their sin is credited to Christ's account even though they do not know this to be the case (though eventually they will). God apparently made such exceptions for Enoch, Job, Melchizedek, Jethro, and others in the Old Testament. The sincere Hindu or Buddhist is also accepted by a Savior he only comes to know at death. Just as children are apparently saved without personal faith in Christ, so others from diverse religions are saved though they have not explicitly believed in Him.

This argument, however, is unconvincing because there is good reason to believe that the men of the Old Testament (referred to above) may indeed have responded to special revelation. There is certainly no evidence that they were followers of some other god. As for the analogy regarding infants, they do not have the ability to respond to the general revelation of nature or conscience. If they go to heaven, as we believe they do, it is because God graciously credits their sins to Christ's account. But there is a difference between those who cannot hear and those who could hear if the opportunity were afforded them.

Cornelius is often used as an example of someone who was converted without direct faith in Christ. He was a devout man who feared God with all his household. Peter, you will recall, was given a vision that corresponded with one also received by Cornelius. When they met and Peter realized that God intended to save this man, he said, "I most certainly understand now that God is not one to show partiality, but in every nation the man who fears Him and does what is right, is welcome to Him" (Acts 10:34–35).

Should we interpret this, as some do, that those who fear God, no matter what their religion, are accepted by Him? Sanders writes, "Cornelius was already a saved believer *before* Peter arrived, but he was not a Christian believer."[2] From this he concludes that some people are saved though they are not Christians.

Again this interpretation appears flawed. For one thing, as Gary Phillips points out in an article entitled, "Evangelical Pluralism: A Singular Problem," New Testament God-fearers believed in the truth of propitiatory sacrifice and Cornelius had already responded to special revelation (Acts 10:3–6).[3] For another, the text says that he was not saved until Peter preached the Word to him (Acts 11:14). Finally, and most important, we must interpret Peter's remark in light of the context: He had just experienced a vision convincing him that Gentiles are also included in the plan of salvation. When he says that God does not show partiality but accepts other God-fearers, he is not saying that they are saved independent of the gospel. He is simply stating what to him was a radical idea; namely, that anyone, even Gentiles, can be saved by responding to the gospel.

Some would disagree with Pinnock in some respects and agree with him in others. But both he and Sanders use two principles of interpretation that almost certainly guarantee the outcome of what they are looking for. The first is that our idea of fairness should largely control what we believe regarding the fate of those who do not know Christ as Savior.

It is lamentable, I think, that Sanders would say that God *must* have some special arrangement for the unevangelized and if not, He would be less worthy of worship, and less just and loving than humans.[4] Obviously by this criteria God should not allow earthquakes, famines, and wars since any sensitive human being would prevent such atrocities if it were within his power. This is bad reasoning and bad theology.

It is dangerous to use our understanding of fairness to control the outcome of our biblical interpretations. Gary Phillips is right when he comments,

> Once fairness is used as a criterion (and exceptions inevitably tend to proliferate) other inequities besides ignorance vie for attention: some may have heard the gospel from a parent who abused them, or from a pastor who later committed adultery. Others may be told about Christ from someone whose intellectual abilities did not commend Christianity as a faith for thoughtful people. Still others are unfortunate enough to have wealth—a tremendous hindrance to salvation. . . . All of these, through no fault of their own, would be negatively disposed toward the gospel. . . . [5]

The point is clear: Every human being can give some reason why he or she rejected the gospel because something or someone was "unfair." We'd all like to rewrite what the Bible says about God to make Him fair. We've all thought of what we would do if we were God to minimize the suffering of human beings in this life and in the one to come. The problem, of course, is that we are not God.

Clark Pinnock is an example of what happens when the Bible is interpreted to make it consistent with "fairness." Years ago he abandoned Calvinism (with its emphasis on God's sovereign choice in salvation, which he deemed unfair) in favor of Arminianism with its emphasis on free will. Then he moved away from traditional Arminianism and opted for a belief in a finite God; a God who does not even know the future! He argued that if God knows who will be saved and who will be lost, the future is in some sense fixed. Thus Pinnock's God does not elect people on any basis because He does not even know who will be saved and who will be lost.

Pinnock thinks God took a risk when He created the world and gave men free will, that God does not know the decisions of free men in advance. He writes that "genuine novelty can appear in history which cannot even be predicted by God."[6] This ignorance on God's part, Pinnock believes, makes the gospel appear more credible, more "fair."

Pinnock is not finished yet. Once the premise was granted that God had to be "fair," he adopted the view that those who are sincere in other religions can be saved without faith in Christ. And, if they are not saved in this life, they can ask for mercy in the life to come. Anyone who stands before God in judgment and asks God for mercy will receive it. God's books, we are told, are never closed. And if there are still some wicked left who have not availed themselves of all these opportunities, fairness requires that they be annihilated rather than consciously suffer forever.[7]

With that in mind we should not be surprised that he writes:

> When we approach the man of a faith other than our own, it will be in a spirit of expectancy to find how God has been speaking to him and what new understanding of the grace and love of God we may ourselves discover in this encounter. Our first task in approaching another people, another culture, another religion is to take off the shoes, for the place we are approaching is holy. Else we find ourselves treading on men's dreams. More seriously still, we may forget that God was here before our arrival.[8]

Pinnock sees other religions as in transition, and thus Christians have opportunities to aid them in seeking truth through dialogue. "God the Logos has more going on by way of redemption than what happened in first-century Palestine."[9] Incredibly, Pinnock appears to depreciate the Incarnation in favor of a universal logos which is at work in all religions. (Is this the cosmic Christ who indwells everyone?)

Our idea of fairness is based on a limited understanding of God's purposes; God may have a different agenda. Isaiah put it this way, "'For My thoughts are not your thoughts, Neither are your ways My ways,' declares the Lord. 'For as the heavens are higher than the earth, So are My ways higher than your ways, And My thoughts than your thoughts'" (Isaiah 55:8–9).

Second, for Pinnock and Sanders, a *possible* interpretation of a text is taken as the *probable* interpretation if it fits with their commitment to "fairness." As Gary Phillips says, "speculations are often rather suddenly taught as certainties; a *remote* interpretation of a text is taken as the *real* interpretation."[10]

We have no right to be more broadminded than God. To quote Gary Phillips once more, we "would rather err on the side of safety than gamble on speculative leniency."[11] We cannot go beyond what God has revealed. If He has a plan to save those of other religions, He has not seen fit to reveal it to us.

THE FAITH IN CHRIST VIEW

I believe that the Scriptures require us to view other religions as the flawed attempts of man to reach God through human effort and insight. Paul makes two points about paganism. First, he says that those who worship idols actually are worshiping demons:

> No, but I say that the things which the Gentiles sacrifice, they sacrifice to demons, and not to God; and I do not want you to become sharers in demons. You cannot drink the cup of the Lord and the cup of demons; you cannot partake of the table of the Lord and the table of demons. (1 Corinthians 10:20–21)

He does not say that the Gentiles (pagans) are really worshiping God in their own way. All religion is either worship of the true God or idolatry. Read these passages from the Old Testament and ask yourself whether we should reverently take the shoes from off our feet in the presence of pagan worship. "And you shall tear down their altars and smash their sacred pillars and burn their Asherim with fire, and you shall cut down the engraved images of their gods, and you shall obliterate their name from that place" (Deuteronomy 12:3). And again, "For all the gods of the peoples are idols, But the Lord made the heavens"

(Psalm 96:5). Elijah, in the presence of the prophets of Baal, certainly did not think he was standing on holy ground.

Second, Paul taught that religions evolved because man did not honor the true God. Because of rebellion, they "exchanged the glory of the incorruptible God for an image in the form of corruptible man and of birds and four-footed animals and crawling creatures" (Romans 1:23). Satan orchestrated false religions, offering a smorgasbord of options, but all of them stand against the gospel of Christ.

In the first chapter, I referred to the blind men of Indostan who investigated an elephant, and each came to a different conclusion as to how the beast should be described. The point made by some is that different religions are simply different aspects of the same reality. Now we realize that the different religions do not even describe the same elephant (i.e., the same God). Little wonder they come up with contradictory attributes of whatever gods or goddesses there be!

Even those who seek the true God (and there are some who do) cannot come to any saving knowledge of the Almighty without the light of revelation. On Mars Hill Paul said that God determined the appointed times of the nations of the earth and their boundaries "that they should seek God, if perhaps they might grope for Him and find Him, though He is not far from each one of us" (Acts 17:27). Then he went on to urge them to believe in the God who raised Christ from the dead. Without the light of revelation the best man could do is to grope for understanding, straining for a hint of hope and means of forgiveness.

In the New Testament, hearing comes before believing, "Truly, truly, I say to you, he who hears My word, and believes Him who sent Me, has eternal life, and does not come into judgment, but has passed out of death into life" (John 5:24). Paul clarified the sequence when he wrote, "How then shall they call upon Him in whom they have not believed? And how shall they believe in Him whom they have not heard? And how shall they hear without a preacher? . . . So faith comes from hearing, and hearing by the word of Christ" (Romans 10:14, 17).

The apostles stressed that it is through His name alone that salvation comes, "And there is salvation in no one else; for there is no other name under heaven that has been given among men, by which we must be saved" (Acts 4:12). Christ, in what is known as the Great Commission, implies that people have to hear the gospel before they will be saved. We simply have no clear example of salvation apart from a knowledge of Christ.

I do not deny that there might be some good ethical teaching in other religions. Buddhism in particular stresses a form of selfless devotion that appears to have something in common with Christianity. We should expect this, since all people are created in the image of God and have a moral consciousness. But all these religions fail at the most central point; namely, the question of how sinners can be reconciled to God. In the end, if they worship at all, they worship another god.

Regardless of how much we would want to see non-Christians saved, we must be cautious about being more lenient than the biblical teaching. We must worship God as He is and not the God we, given our finite understanding, would want Him to be.

GOD'S BASIS FOR JUDGMENT

Our sentiments must be set aside when they conflict with God's revelation. The Almighty has given us enough information to satisfy our minds but not enough to satisfy our hearts. Since we are not privy to all His hidden purposes, we cannot give a comprehensive answer to this question of the lostness of men and women. But we do have some revelation that will guide us.

1. *Everyone will be judged on the basis of knowledge.*

Specifically, when the unconverted stand before God, every hidden detail will be brought to light to ascertain exactly what was done with what was known. "For all who have sinned without the Law will also perish without the Law; and all who have sinned under the Law will be judged by the Law. . . . For when Gentiles who do not have the Law do instinctively the things of the Law, these, having not the Law, are a law to themselves, in that they show the work of the Law written on their hearts, their conscience bearing witness, and their thoughts alternately accusing or else defending them" (Romans 2:12, 14–15).

Jews will be judged on the basis of the law revealed on Sinai and Gentiles will be judged by conscience, the law of God written on their hearts. As F. F. Bruce said, they will be "judged by the light that is available, not by the light that is unavailable." But of course we must hasten to add that no Jew has ever lived up to the Law of Moses and no Gentile has ever lived up to the light of conscience. The verdict of God is clear: *All have sinned and come short of the glory of God.*

It is quite possible (and missionaries often report) that those who have earnestly sought more light have received it. If there are such, it is because God is at work in their hearts. When the gospel message comes they say, "This is what I was waiting for." I doubt, however, that we have enough information to say that in each instance more light has come even when people have sought the true God. Missionary stories are enlightening but do not provide a basis for a final theological position on the issue. There are some things (perhaps many) that we simply do not know.

2. *General revelation is a basis for judgment, but not a basis for salvation.*

If you need $1,000 for college and I give you only $100, my gift is not enough to get you into college, but it is enough to judge your response. With this $100 I can tell whether you love me or spurn me. And how you respond may determine whether or not you ever receive the full amount.

Christ, when speaking a parable about the need for faithfulness, said, "And that slave who knew his master's will and did not get ready or act in accord with his will, shall receive many lashes, but the one who did not know it, and committed deeds worthy of a flogging, will receive but few. And from everyone who has been given much shall much be required; and to whom they entrusted much, of him they will ask all the more" (Luke 12:47–48). We can be sure that (1) there will be degrees of punishment commensurate with knowledge; and, (2) that every bit of information about the circumstance and inner heart response will be taken into account. God's knowledge will be detailed, balanced, and complete.

Our works do not save us, but for the unsaved works are the basis of judgment ". . . and the dead were judged from the things which were written in the books, according to their deeds" (Revelation 20:12). Those who did good works but did not trust Christ will be lost, for God cannot accept sinners into His presence without a payment for their sins. But their judgment will be less severe than those who defied conscience and rebelled against the outer light of nature and the inner light of conscience. But the judgment will be fair; there will be no false accusations; no relevant fact will be overlooked.

People who speak glibly today about the innate goodness of mankind and our ability to usher in Utopia violate both the light of nature (which reveals a God of power) and their conscience (which reveals their sin and great need of divine help). Anyone in a moment of reflective honesty would have to admit that he is helpless to deal with the alienation and sin that exists within every heart. Standing before God, everyone will have to admit that he knew better.

Justice, I believe, will be so accurately distributed, so delicately balanced that throughout all eternity we will sing "Righteous and true are Thy ways" (Revelation 15:3b). I believe that even those who are lost—yes, even the devil himself—will have to confess throughout all of eternity that what God did was just and right. God never commits an injustice.

3. *God is under no obligation to save those who have never heard of Christ.*

Is God fair? The earthquake in California that kills 60 people or the one in India that kills 40,000 seems patently unfair. Yet will anyone deny that it was God who predetermined that these calamities would happen? He was, after all, the creator of the earth's crust; He has determined where it would be weak and where it would be strong. Even if (as Pinnock and other Arminians would want to argue) God only permitted it, why didn't He choose to not permit it? Surely you and I would have prevented this tragedy if it were within our power to do so.

When Paul argues that God even uses His power to harden some hearts and soften others, the apostle is well aware that his readers (us included) will regard the Almighty's actions as unfair. So he asks the question that is on everyone's mind, "You will say to me then, 'Why does He still find fault? For who resists His will?'" (Romans 9:19).

Of course we expect him to launch into a defense of God; we anticipate reasons why God's idea of fairness is, in the final analysis, close to ours. But he rejects such reasoning and asserts:

> On the contrary, who are you, O man, who answers back to God? The thing molded will not say to the molder, "Why did you make me like this," will it? Or does not the potter have a right over the clay, to make from the same lump one vessel for honorable use, and another for common use? What if God, although willing to demonstrate His wrath and to make His power known, endured with much patience vessels of wrath prepared for destruction? And He did so in order that He might make known the riches of His glory upon vessels of mercy, which He prepared beforehand for glory. (Romans 9:20–23)

Paul makes two telling points. First, that there is no standard independent of God by which the Almighty is to be judged. God does not have to conform to our standard of fairness, though He must be fair in keeping with His nature and long-range objectives. Within these parameters, He is free to do as He pleases.

If we say, as some do, that it would be unfair for God to require eternal punishment for sins committed over a relatively short period of a few years, we can do no better than to quote the words of Jonathan Edwards:

> Our obligation to love, honor and obey any being is in proportion to his loveliness, honorableness and authority. . . . But God is a being infinitely lovely, because he hath infinite excellency and beauty. . . . So a sin against God, being a violation of infinite obligations, must be a crime infinitely heinous, and so deserving infinite punishment. . . . The eternity of the punishment of the ungodly men renders it infinite . . . and therefore renders it no more than proportionate to the heinousness of what they are guilty of.[12]

John Piper points out that the infinite horrors of hell are a vivid demonstration of the infinite value of the glory of God which sinners have belittled. Infinite punishment rests on those who are infinitely guilty. What if the greatness of the sin is determined by the greatness of the God against whom it is committed?[13] Paul asked, "What shall we say, then? There is no injustice with God, is there? May it never be!" (Romans 9:14). Yes, even if we were lost, God would be fair.

Second, Paul argues that God displays His justice and wrath in His dealings with the ungodly, but His mercy and grace are given to those who believe. He is not obligated to treat everyone alike. When Paul speaks of God's impartiality (Romans 2:11), the context is the day of judgment when the unbelieving world will be judged by the same standard, namely knowledge and performance.

In this life, God does not treat everyone alike. He did not appear to Hammurabi as He appeared to Abraham; Christ appeared to Paul en route to Damascus in a way that He did not appear to Pilate. We have a world of people who have unequal ability, unequal opportunity, and unequal life spans. In some God displays His mercy, in others His justice. This is simply the way God has chosen to run His world. He can do this and be fair.

Is it not dangerous, or possibly even presumptuous, to insist that God must conform to our thinking or else we will withhold our unreserved adoration? William Cowper wrote of those who would revise God's providential plan:

They take from God's hand the balance and the rod
They rejudge His justice and become the judge of God.

OTHER RELIGIONS AND GOD'S LOVE

The fact that God does not owe salvation to everyone (indeed, He does not owe it to anyone) still troubles us because we ask, "Would not a loving God have arranged the world in such a way that more people could have taken advantage of

Christ's supreme work?" Love, one would think, would have overcome any barriers that exist to the salvation of all men.

However, God has a bigger plan than we can see; He has an eternal purpose which led Him to choose this world and its arrangements. If we ask why He does not save more than He did, we must answer that He has a plan that we can't see; He has a plan that desires to augment His own glory. We exist for Him; He does not exist for us. The wrath of man is made to please Him. J. L. Monsabre wrote, "If God would concede to me His omnipotence for 24 hours, you would see how many changes I would make in the world. But if He gave me His wisdom too, I would leave things as they are."

The theologian Warfield points out that the love of God must of necessity be under the control of His righteousness and His eternal purposes. In answer to those who ask why God doesn't save more people, Warfield says that the old answer is still the best one: "God in His love saves as many of the guilty race of man as he can get the consent of his whole nature to save."[14] His eternal objectives must be taken into account.

If God has a plan to save men and women without personal faith in Christ, He has not seen fit to reveal it. We must resist the temptation to make the Scriptures say what we think they should. Our role is to spread the gospel with the firm conviction that faith comes by hearing and that people cannot believe what they do not know.

But how can we believe this doctrine—which is so contrary to everything our culture believes—and not be tagged with arrogance? How do we fulfill the Great Commission in light of the urgency of the message?

We now turn our attention to the responsibility and privilege God has shared with us. We have a part in His grand plan for the world.

NOTES

1. Raymond Panikkar, *The Unknown Christ of Hinduism* (City: Darton, Longman and Todd, 1965), 54.
2. John Sanders, *No Other Name* (Grand Rapids: Eerdmans, 1992), 208.
3. W. Gary Phillips, "Evangelical Pluralism: A Singular Problem," *Bibliotheca Sacra*, April-June, 1994), 11.
4. Sanders, *No Other Name*, xvii,3,6.
5. Phillips, "Pluralism," 12.
6. "Clark Pinnock's Response" in *Predestination and Free Will*, eds. David Basinger and Randall Basinger (Downer's Grove, Ill: InterVarsity, 1986), 150.
7. Clark Pinnock, *A Wideness in God's Mercy: The Finality of Jesus Christ in a World of Religions* (Grand Rapids: Zondervan, 1992), 98, 111, 158, 172–76.
8. Ibid., 141.
9. Ibid., 77.
10. Phillips, "Pluralism," 11.
11. Ibid., 15.
12. Quoted in *Let the Nations Be Glad* by John Piper, (Grand Rapids: Baker, 1993), 128.
13. Ibid., 127.
14. Frank Mead, ed., *12,000 Religious Quotations* (Grand Rapids: Baker, 1989), 179.

AN
EXTRAORDINARY
RESPONSIBILITY—

How Can We Best Represent Him?

On a wall near the main entrance to the Alamo in San Antonio, Texas, hung a portrait with this inscription:

James Butler Bonham—no picture of him exists. This portrait is of his nephew Major James Bonham, now deceased, who greatly resembles his uncle. It was placed here by his family that people might know the appearance of the man who died for freedom.

Likewise no portrait of Christ exists, but His resemblance should be seen in the lives of His followers. We are called to stand in for Him during this period when He is "waiting until His enemies become His footstool."

All believers are His representatives whether faithful or unfaithful; courageous or cowardly. Our challenge is to represent Him as best we can, both with our lives and with our lips. As Peter wrote, "But even if you should suffer for the sake of righteousness, you are blessed. And do not fear their intimidation, and do not be troubled, but sanctify Christ as Lord in your hearts, always being ready to make a defense to everyone who asks you to give an account for the hope that in in you; yet with gentleness and reverence" (1 Peter 3:14–15).

How can we be active witnesses for Christ in an era of unprecedented tolerance, an era in which converting someone else to your religious views is labeled bigotry and prejudice? If tolerance is indeed a national icon, how can we witness without the stigma of self-righteousness and a penchant for doctrinal hair-splitting? How can we represent the exclusivity of Christ at a time when the very idea of exclusivity is what turns people off?

To begin, I must remind us (as I tried to point out in chapter 2) that there is no necessary connection between exclusivism and intolerance. Though we must hold uncompromisingly to the essentials of our biblical faith, we should be models of gracious tolerance and humble open-mindedness.

In his excellent book, *Dissonant Voices,* Harold Netland gives a helpful explanation of the three kinds of tolerance. *Legal tolerance* is a basic acceptance of everyone's right to whatever religion (or lack of one) they choose. In many Western democracies, such tolerance is specifically written into the constitution. Americans are well-acquainted with the phrase, "Congress shall make no law respecting the establishment of religion nor prohibiting the free exercise thereof."

Such tolerance is a recognition of the basic human right to practice one's own religious tradition (or none at all). We must stand in opposition to the medieval unity of church and state where heretics were burned at the stake, killed with the sword, or drowned. Unfortunately, the church of medieval Europe was influenced by pagan Rome which confused political patriotism with religious commitment. The idea that Christ's followers should be like sheep among the wolves was largely lost in the religious/political power struggles of that era.

Today, freedom of religion (religious tolerance, if you please) is denied in Muslim countries were it is illegal to try to persuade others to accept another faith. Converts to Christianity are often jailed, tortured, or even put to death. The religions of the Far East often give an aura of tolerance that is particularly directed toward Western audiences. However, those who have lived in countries where Hinduism or Buddhism are predominant tell stories of repression, persecution, and ostracism for those who abandon a given religion and opt for another faith.

As Christians we must fight for legal tolerance; that is, the freedom for individuals to believe as they wish. No one can be coerced to believe in Christ; no one should be rejected because he belongs to another religion. The true church has always been a minority within society—politically weak, but spiritually strong.

Second, there is *social tolerance.* This means that we treat other people with respect regardless of their religious views. We believe that all people are created in the image of God and therefore have dignity and worth. This kind of tolerance is a demonstration of Christian love, a willingness to love others, even those whom we believe to be wrong.

The third kind of tolerance is *intellectual;* that is, the question of whether one is willing to compromise his fundamental beliefs. As this book was intended to demonstrate, the committed Christian cannot tolerate other views, if by tolerance we mean accepting the beliefs of other religions. Those who dialogue with other religions with the intention of integrating such beliefs with Christianity redefine truth and weaken the message of the gospel.

Let's not be intimidated by the politically correct view that no one should ever be expected to hear something with which he disagrees! We certainly should be willing to listen to people of other religions to better understand them and their faith. Nor should we be offended if they seek to convert us to their points of view. Dialogue to gain understanding is necessary and Christian; dialogue to synthesize beliefs is neither.

Nor does tolerance mean that we should never say anything negative about another religion or belief. Every person of whatever religion should have the right to judge and critically evaluate other beliefs. The time, place, and attitude we adopt are all important, but sharing our faith and contrasting it with others has to become a normal part of our experience. The proliferation of other religions in the United States provides us with an unprecedented opportunity. Tozer said, "The half-converted may shy away from the bigotry and intolerance that he fears lie in an exclusive devotion to Christianity, but the wholly converted will have no such apprehensions. . . . To him there is none other name under heaven given among men whereby we must be saved."

Evangelism is not proselytism, which by definition is coercive and manipulative. Evangelism communicates a message and seeks to persuade others to believe it, but it must never violate the dignity of the listeners or become manipulative. The truth must always be spoken in love. We can be inclusive in our friendships, but we must be exclusive in our commitment to the truth.

To clarify: We must distinguish between respecting a person and accepting his belief system. We can model legal and social tolerance and still seek to persuade others to believe in Christ. To quote Netland, "Being tolerant of others in different religious traditions then, does not entail accepting their basic beliefs as true, or even the refusal to make any kind of judgment about the content of their basic beliefs."[1]

Even the world at large agrees that uncritical tolerance is not always a virtue. Netland points out that the man who passively watches while several other men gang rape a helpless woman will not be praised for his tolerance. Similarly, never to disagree with anyone, though we believe they have accepted doctrines that will lead them to hell, can hardly be called a virtue.[2]

Our *attitude* is key. We must learn how to present our beliefs with conviction and yet treat others with courtesy, love, and respect. Peter says we should share our faith "with meekness and fear." The humility of Christ is our example.

Suppose you were not a Christian: Knowing what you know about the destiny of those who die without personal faith in Christ, how concerned do you wish someone else would be to present the gospel to you? To what lengths would you want others to go to bring you the only message that can save you? Remember that the people we are concerned about are just as valuable as we ourselves are. Put yourself in their shoes and ask, "What do we owe them?"

Yet, as John Piper points out, not even the lostness of man should be our overriding motivation for evangelism. He writes,

"Missions is not the ultimate goal of the church. Worship is. Missions exists because worship doesn't. Worship is ultimate, not missions because God is ultimate, not man."[3] Our burning passion should be for more people to worship the Christ whom we adore. We must look at our friends not as "souls to be saved" but as people who potentially could be redeemed and enrolled in the gallery of His worshipers.

So how do we share the gospel, free of self-righteousness and repulsive intolerance of the worst sort? We can begin by simply telling our testimony, explaining why we have believed in Christ and why we personally have come to faith in His credibility. We must never give the impression that we are exempt from the failings and struggles of others; the more human we are, the more powerful our witness will be.

Of course we must, as best we can, answer objections to the Christian faith. And yet, again and again we must point to Christ and His qualifications as the source of what we believe. We cannot draw attention to ourselves lest we be like one person who lamented a breakdown in communication by saying, "I pointed to the moon, but all you saw was my finger."

Think of how Christ adapted His witness to His audience and yet never infringed on the boundaries of respect. We have been called to represent Him: We are His ambassadors, asked to live and speak on His behalf. To the Father He said, "As Thou didst send Me into the world, I also have sent them into the world" (John 17:18).

STANDING IN CHRIST'S STEAD

Like our Savior, we are sent into the world; there is no room for a monastery in a New Testament faith. Whenever the gospel has found its mark, it has left the cloister and gone into the marketplace. The cry of the Reformation was the cry to return the living faith of ordinary people into the world.

To speak on behalf of the queen or the president of the United States is both an honor and a coveted responsibility. To speak on behalf of Christ is the most grand vision ever to enter the human spirit. We will never recover the impact of the Christian faith until we have a revival of the laity, a firm commitment that every vocation is sacred; every believer is on duty for His King.

Christ, as we have learned, is wholly different from us in His deity; yet He is like us in His humanity and in His mission. He was sent, we are sent. There are similarities in the sending process.

We Are Sent Purposefully

We are sent into the world for the specific purpose of communicating a message. Christianity must compete in the marketplace of ideas. We must engage our culture in discussion and debate. Informal dialogue, answering questions, etc. is a part of the process. So are kindness, compassion, and a commitment to friendship. How can we expect our friends to accept Christ if there is no willingness on our part to listen to their views, appreciate their objections, and understand their personal differences with our message?

On Mars Hill Paul pointed to an inscription, "To an unknown god," and then declared that it was this God whom he was proclaiming to the philosophers who gathered to hear him. He knew that even those who were steeped in paganism were created in the image of God and sought religious truth to fill the void. Though the God whom Paul proclaimed had no common ground with the gods of the Athenians, Paul's means of communication found common ground with his listeners.

More people are ready to listen to the message of Christ than we are aware of. We are here for the purpose of connecting the message with those who may be ready to hear.

We Are Sent Dependently

Though Christ was God, He did not use His attributes but set them aside to live as a human being. Suppose you were a millionaire but chose to live and work with the poorest of the poor. At any time you could write a check and leave the ghetto, but you do not depend upon your considerable resources. Even so Christ, who had every right to be exempt from the limitations of humanity, refused to draw on His divine resources but depended on the Father for His strength.

This explains why Christ, who possessed all the attributes of deity, spent whole nights in prayer. The Father gave Him the power to live and the words to speak. He never felt abandoned even when the results of His work appeared small or when the people He cared about became angry with Him.

Does the prospect of witnessing to your next door neighbor frighten you? Are you intimidated with the thought that you will not know what to say or will be considered weird? Or, do you think that the unconverted are so hard-hearted that they would never believe on Christ anyway?

We are not alone in the soul-saving business. When Christ wanted to teach Peter about fishing for men, He commanded fish to stay away from his nets during the night when they would normally be caught; then He commanded them (contrary to their usual custom) to swim into Peter's net in the morning. The reason: Christ wanted to prove that when we fish for men we are not alone! Behind our own attempts to witness are the purpose, power, and providential work of God.

Remember it is not our responsibility to convert anyone. We do what is *possible;* namely, plant the seeds of the gospel in the human heart; God does the *impossible;* namely, plant faith and life in the human heart.

We Are Sent Joyfully

Was the career of Christ one of suffering or joy? Of course it was both, for suffering and joy are not opposites. In Hebrews we read, ". . . who for the joy set before Him endured the cross . . ." (Hebrews 12:2).

This joy involved saying no to the natural human inclinations to avoid pain and opt for a life of ease. Looked at in one way, Christ was most pleased to come to redeem us; yet from another standpoint we read, "Even Christ pleased not himself." Note this well: Christ had to set aside His desire to please Himself in order that He might please the Father (John 8:29).

Joy and sorrow are not opposites. They co-existed in the life of Christ and in ours as well. Samuel Zwemer, famous for his missionary work among the Muslims, did not see many converts during his years of work in the Persian Gulf. The temperatures often soared to 107 degrees, and in 1904 both of his daughters died within a few days of each other. Nevertheless, fifty years later he looked back upon his trials and wrote, "The sheer joy of it all comes back. Gladly would I do it all over again."

Representing Christ, for all its difficulties, is a joy indeed.

We Are Sent "Unitedly"

Christ prayed for "the men whom Thou gavest me out of the world" (John 17:6). After He ascended, the disciples met together in the Upper Room to receive the Holy Spirit that they might be made members of the same body. This unity was the secret of their powerful witness. One of the purposes of the body of Christ, the local congregation, is to provide the encouragement and training needed to effectively represent Christ in our world. The reason the early church had such a major impact in the ancient world is that they were in "one accord" in their witness. We are strengthened by men and women who know the same Christ.

We Are Sent Triumphantly

Was Christ's mission accomplished? At first it would seem no since so few, relatively speaking, believed on Him. The official religious establishment crucified Christ. Yet, Christ could say that He had "finished the work that the Father had given Him to do." The seeds had been sown, the church had been established, and those whom the Father had given to Christ had come, just as promised.

Look through the pages of church history and you will find that the church has had many periods of decline and expansion. It has suffered through persecution, innumerable heresies, and division and failure. Yet, in and through and in spite of human failure, the divine will has been accomplished.

Given the proliferation of false religions, the distortions of the gospel, and the moral and spiritual decline in the West, it is easy to conclude that the purpose of God is failing in the world. But this would be to profoundly misunderstand the biblical doctrine of divine providence. Nothing is happening which God did not expect to have happen; or better, nothing is happening in the world which is not a part of the divine plan.

Christ predicted that the end of the age would be characterized by anarchy and deception. There would be wars, famine, and earthquakes. His people will be hated by all nations on account of His name. There will be unparalleled deceptions and lawlessness. These things must come to pass.

Where is the triumph? "All the ends of the earth will remember and turn to the Lord, And all the families of the nations will worship before Thee. For the kingdom is the Lord's, and He rules over the nations" (Psalm 22:27–28). This prediction will be fulfilled in the Millennium, but it is our assurance that the purposes of God will never fail. Yes, the knowledge of the Lord will yet cover the earth as waters cover the sea.

Those whom Christ purchased will be redeemed, "Worthy art Thou to take the book and to break its seals; for Thou wast slain, and didst purchase for God with Thy blood men from every tribe and tongue and people and nation" (Revelation 5:9).

The purposes of God are on track and we have been called to be a part of His worldwide program. Ultimate, eternal success is inevitable.

THE MARCHING ORDERS

When Christ was about to ascend into heaven, He gave final instructions: "All authority has been given to Me in heaven and on earth. Go therefore and make disciples of all the nations, baptizing them in the name of the Father and the Son and the Holy Spirit, teaching them to observe all that I commanded you; and lo, I am with you always, even to the end of the age" (Matthew 28:18–20).

Let's consider four universal statements Christ gives here.

Christ Has All Authority

To believe that Christ has all authority in heaven is, of course, not difficult. We've already learned that His presence there changed the character of heaven forever. Nor is it difficult to believe that Christ has all authority on earth in a general sense. Christ presides over the present rebellion "waiting until His enemies be made a footstool for His feet." What is more difficult for some people to accept is that His authority even extends to the human will. Does He have the authority to take even hardened hearts and give them the ability to believe on Him?

Yes, of course He has such power. To His Father He prayed, ". . . even as Thou gavest Him authority over all mankind, that to all whom Thou has given Him, He may give eternal life" (John 17:2). Elsewhere He assures us that "All that the Father gives Me shall come to Me, and the one who comes to Me I will certainly not cast out" (John 6:37).

This should encourage those who are witnesses, even in countries that are hostile in their opposition to the Christian faith. This should encourage us to witness to neighbors and friends who seem either disinterested or steeped in a form of religion that blinds the mind and hardens the heart. We must not suppose that anyone is beyond the possibility of conversion for the simple reason that the human heart is, in the final analysis, in God's hand. The Holy Spirit is well-qualified to overcome opposition to the gospel message. There is no chance that the ultimate purpose of God will fail.

You and I do not have the right to judge whom God might choose to save or not save. No one exists outside the umbrella of Christ's authority. He is able to give men and women the gift of repentance which results in the gift of eternal life. "All authority has been given unto Me."

Our Responsibility Includes All Nations

This is a big assignment that includes all nations geographically. Since Christ is presented as the only qualified Savior for all the peoples of the earth, He is not the Savior of the West while there is another Savior for the East.

Unfortunately we can become very limited in our vision. We can be glad that the gospel is for our families, for our friends and relatives. Possibly our burden even extends to the whole United States. But if God is interested in a nation of 300 million, is He not also interested in India with its 700 million and China with its billion?

We must become world Christians; that is, believers who have a heart that extends beyond our immediate geographical limitations. Why should one part of the earth receive all of our attention? Surely we have not more intrinsic value than people in other countries and those of other religions. Blessed is the person with a heart for the world.

This also means "all nations" religiously. What percentage of the world's population is Christian? Of course, any figure can only be an estimate, not only because we are not qualified to count all the individual congregations but also because we cannot judge human hearts. Although about half the world's population can be loosely called Christian, about 9 percent adhere to some kind of doctrinal understanding of the gospel. But in the end, perhaps only 1 or 2 percent of the world's population has "savingly believed." The largest percentage has always been found in the United States and Canada, but that is now changing. The emerging churches in Central America and the far east (Korea, for example) are shifting the critical mass of the church.

We must not be intimidated by the growth of other religions in our own country. In the final congregation of the redeemed there will be representatives of all countries and former followers of all the various religions. The triumph of Christ is certain, and even in this era we can have a part in His victory.

We Are to Teach All Things

Evangelism is only the first step in making disciples. Growth and development takes time and training. Christ showed us how to make disciples, welding a group of men into a small spiritual army that eventually spread the gospel throughout the world.

The challenge is to deepen our understanding of truth and our own commitment to it. Since we can only take people as far as we ourselves have gone, it is important that we grow in our own discipleship that we might affect others, teaching "all things" Christ commanded.

Christ Is with Us Always

Christ is not only the universal Savior, but He has a universal presence. Wherever we go, we can be sure that He is there ahead of us, preparing for our arrival, and continuing His work after we leave. He is with us in our victories and He stands beside us in our defeats. Whenever a person comes to trust Him as Savior, we know that He is at work, performing a miracle in the human heart.

And when we present the gospel and see no evidence of saving faith, we must remember that He is there also. When the believers in Rome were discouraged because the Jews did not accept Christ as Savior, Paul confronted the question directly. Had God failed? He writes, "But it is not as though the word of God has failed" (Romans 9:6). He goes on to assure believers that the purposes of God are on target. Nothing—not even the hard hearts of unbelievers—falls outside the boundaries of divine providence. In the end God will always win.

James Stephens attended Sunday school as a child, but when he went to college he became a Buddhist. He was told he could change himself through discipline and instruction. He says that the chanting in the meetings sounded like the angels in heaven. For fourteen years he was so zealous that he won fifty-four converts over to Buddhism. He practiced self-denial as the means to enlightenment and as best he could followed the eight-fold path. He directed his chanting toward a piece of paper called "the Gohonzon," which was the object of his worship.

Eventually, he became disenchanted with his religion. First, he was disillusioned because of broken promises—the change of heart did not happen. In fact he said, "I was noticing in my heart more depravity to the point where I could scarcely identify with a pure conscience." He admitted he was living a lie. Instead of peace, he found emptiness. When he asked for answers, he was simply told that he should do more religious things. He was increasingly dissatisfied.

Second, a friend gave him some Christian books and a Bible. When he read the gospel of John, he says it was "utterly different from the Christ that Buddhist leaders told us about." He discovered that Christ was a living Master, One who was not reincarnated but resurrected. This God was not a force as his previous gods purported to be, but the person who created him and loved him.

He read the words, "I am the bread of life. He who comes to me will never go hungry, and he who believes in me will never be thirsty" (John 6:35 NIV). He says, "Convicted of my sin against a holy God, I laid my burden at the Savior's feet and gave Him my life. That night my wife, a Nichiren Shoshu Buddhist for 16 years, also believed and was saved. What grace."

And in the end, that is the difference between Christ and other gods. His grace is given in the midst of our *dis*grace. He is the Savior who doesn't just point the way, but takes us where we need to go.

> To Him who loves us, and released us from our sins by His blood, and He has made us to be a kingdom, priests to His God and Father; to Him be the glory and the dominion forever and ever. Amen. (Revelation 1:5b–6)

Amen!

NOTES

1. Harold Netland, *Dissonant Voices* (Grand Rapids: Eerdmans, 1991), 309.
2. Ibid., 305
3. John Piper, *Let The Nations Be Glad* (Grand Rapids: Baker, 1993), 11.

Other Books by Erwin Lutzer